Uncomplicating

ALGEBRA

*to Meet Common Core
Standards in Math, K–8*

Uncomplicating
ALGEBRA
to Meet Common Core
Standards in Math, K–8

MARIAN SMALL

TEACHERS COLLEGE PRESS

TEACHERS COLLEGE | COLUMBIA UNIVERSITY
NEW YORK AND LONDON

NELSON EDUCATION

www.nelson.com

Published by Teachers College Press, 1234 Amsterdam Avenue, New York, NY 10027; distributed in Canada by Nelson Education, 1120 Birchmount Road, Toronto, ON, Canada M1K 5G4.

Text Design: Lynne Frost

Library of Congress Cataloging-in-Publication Data

Small, Marian.
   Uncomplicating algebra to meet common core standards in math, K–8 / Marian Small.
     pages cm
   "Teachers College, Columbia University."
   Includes bibliographical references and index.
   ISBN 978-0-8077-5517-4 (pbk. : alk. paper)
   ISBN 978-0-8077-7309-3 (e-book)
     1. Algebra—Study and teaching (Primary)—Standards—United States.
   2. Algebra—Study and teaching (Elementary)—Standards—United States.
   3. Mathematics—Study and teaching (Primary)—Standards—United States.
   4. Mathematics—Study and teaching (Elementary)—Standards—United States.
   I. Title.
   QA159.S57 2014
   372.7'1021873—dc23   2014000913

ISBN 978-0-8077-5517-4 (paper)
ISBN 978-0-8077-7309-3 (ebook)

Printed on acid-free paper
Manufactured in the United States of America

21 20 19 18 17   8 7 6 5 4 3 2

CONTENTS

PREFACE

ORGANIZATION OF THE BOOK

This resource is intended to help teachers improve student success in learning algebra by sharing approaches that will lead to a deeper and richer understanding of the subject.

The resource is organized by grade level around the Common Core State Standards for Mathematics (CCSSM) that are related to algebraic thinking. The grades covered in this resource begin with Kindergarten, where the first relevant standard is found in the Operations and Algebraic Thinking domain, and end with Grade 8, where the focus is on working with linear equations and functions. For each section, a portion of the relevant standard is presented, followed by a delineation of important underlying ideas associated with that portion of the standard, as well as some Good Questions to Ask to bring those underlying ideas out.

The discussions of underlying ideas include

* background on the mathematics of the standard,
* suggestions for appropriate representations of the specific mathematical ideas,
* suggestions for explaining the ideas to students, and
* cautions about misconceptions or situations to avoid.

Following each set of underlying ideas is a group of Good Questions to Ask that can be used for classroom instruction, student practice, or assessment. Among the questions are many open questions, as well as more directed conceptual questions that might be supplemental to what teachers normally are provided in the resources they use. The Common Core State Standards for Mathematical Practice underlie the content throughout and are explicitly mentioned in a number of instances.

For Whom Is This Book Useful and Why?

This resource is designed to aid math teachers of Kindergarten–Grade 5 in building a solid foundation for student work in algebra in the middle grades and to aid teachers of Grades 6–8 in preparing students for work in algebra in the secondary grades. It is also intended to serve as a resource for math coaches in assisting classroom teachers in their transition to teaching mathematics within the more demanding framework of the Common Core State Standards. I expect this book to be helpful as well to preservice teachers as they prepare themselves to understand and teach math in a way that will foster a deep level of understanding in their students.

Considering the Bigger Picture

While I would hope that all users would read the entire book, I particularly encourage this approach for math coaches and preservice teachers. For grade-level or grade-band teachers, I suggest reading the Introduction and the grade-level sections that most directly apply for their particular groups of students, but also becoming acquainted with the mathematics related to algebra taught in grades directly below and above their groups. Because students in any classroom possess different levels of knowledge, in order to differentiate instruction appropriately, teachers must be aware of missing prerequisite knowledge, as well as suitable directions for moving forward.

Lastly, I hope that using this book helps make algebra make more sense both to the readers and to their students.

ACKNOWLEDGMENTS

I have been fortunate to work with excellent editors in preparing this manuscript. I wish to thank, too, several reviewers whose comments were very helpful in shaping the manuscript. Most importantly, I have been fortunate to have interacted with so many teachers who have responded positively to my approach to mathematics teaching and learning. These educators have continued to encourage me to write more. I thank these professionals for their personal support, as well as for sharing my work with their colleagues.

Uncomplicating
ALGEBRA
*to Meet Common Core
Standards in Math, K–8*

INTRODUCTION

INCREASED FOCUS ON ALGEBRA

Students' success or lack of success in early algebra can have a significant effect on their futures (Usiskin, 1995). Algebra is often required for graduation from high school. It is also seen as a critical course for opening doors for many future careers. In fact, one of the tasks of the National Mathematics Advisory Panel to the president of the United States was to identify the skills needed for students to learn algebra (National Mathematics Advisory Panel, 2008). It is widely accepted that to achieve the current U.S. goal of algebra for all, students in elementary and middle schools must have better preparatory experiences than has historically been the case (Cai & Knuth, 2005).

WHAT IS ALGEBRA?

Although many view algebra as math that you do with letters, the topic of algebra is much more complex than that. There is value in looking at how different researchers define algebra to make sense of how algebra manifests itself in the Common Core State Standards for Mathematics.

For example, Usiskin (1988) described four different notions of what algebra is:

* A way to generalize and formalize arithmetic: for example, using the algebraic equation $ab = ba$ to indicate that any two numbers can be multiplied in either order; or $a(-b) = -ab$ as a means to indicate that the product of any number and the opposite of another one is the opposite of the product of the two numbers; or $\frac{a}{b} \times \frac{c}{d} = \frac{ac}{bd}$ as a way to indicate the rule for multiplying fractions, again no matter what the numerators and denominators are.
* A procedure for solving certain kinds of problems (e.g., problems like this one: If one amount is 50 more than twice another, and the two amounts total 300, what is each amount?).
* The study of relationships among quantities or variables, for example, $a = 2p$ as a means of describing the number of arms, a, of p people; or $P = 2(l + w)$ as a means of describing the perimeter of a rectangle as double the sum of its length and width. Also involved in working with these

relationships is insight into what they imply. For example, knowing that $a = 2p$ tells us that as p increases, so does a. Knowing that $P = 2(l + w)$ tells us that the sum of the length and width of a rectangle must be half its perimeter.

- The study of structures with certain inherent rules, for example, we factor $x^2 - 9$ by using the rules of symbol manipulation.

Some of these approaches to algebra manifest themselves in the CCSSM standards for grades K–8, particularly the generalizing of arithmetic concepts and the study of relationships among quantities and variables. Usiskin's (1988) other notions of algebra tend to be more significant in the secondary grades.

Generalization is a significant focus even in the early grades. It involves a deliberate extension from particular situations and often involves justification. For example, students generalize when they realize that it is not just that $2 + 3 = 3 + 2$ and $5 + 8 = 8 + 5$, but that any two numbers can be added in any order, and understand why. Or a student might notice that both 4×9 and 2×18 are ways to express 36, but then generalize to the concept that when we multiply two numbers to achieve a particular positive whole number product, if one factor increases, the other decreases. Ellis (2007) points out that generalization is complex, often involving reasoning and communication, and that the ability to generalize grows with more and more opportunities to generalize, which often occurs when students work with patterns.

Variables are related in the earlier grades not only when students create formulas using some measurements of a shape to determine other measurements but also when they consider how various groups of numbers relate, for example, how the multiples of 5 relate to the multiples of 10.

The National Council of Teachers of Mathematics (NCTM, 2000) lists four somewhat different organizing themes for algebra: (1) understanding patterns, relations, and functions; (2) representing and analyzing mathematical situations and structures; (3) using mathematical models to represent and understand quantitative relationships; and (4) analyzing change in various contexts. These themes relate to and overlap Usiskin's (1988) notions and manifest themselves clearly in the CCSSM. Work on pattern in Grades 3–5 leads to generalization, a hallmark of algebra. Using equations to describe both numerical and measurement situations even as early as Grade 1 eventually leads to an examination of how variables are related. Consideration of mathematical models and quantitative relationships occurs at almost all grade levels, with significant attention to the meaning of equations. Analyzing change becomes more prominent in the middle grades, where students explore changes in variables, often using tables of values and graphs.

Because the various aspects of algebra touch on so many areas, standards that require algebraic thinking are found in many strands of the CCSSM, including Number and Measurement.

GENERAL REASONS STUDENTS STRUGGLE WITH ALGEBRA

Historically, the separation of arithmetic and algebra in instructional resources and in teacher instruction for Grades K–8 might have unintentionally interfered with student success in algebra. Students did not really look at algebra as a way to generalize the concepts they dealt with in arithmetic, yet that is an important aspect of algebra, as discussed above. It is telling that the CCSSM, which have been formalized fairly recently, use the subdomain of Operations and Algebraic Thinking within the Number strand in Grades K–5, in recognition of the value of helping teachers and students see the interconnection between number and algebra.

Kieran (2004) suggests that there are critical features that must be included in the integration of arithmetic and algebra to lead to student success in algebra. These include

- A focus on looking at relationships between values and not just on calculating answers,
- A focus on the inverse relationships between addition and subtraction, and multiplication and division, to support equation solving,
- A focus on representing problems and not just on solving them
- A focus on the use of variables along with numbers from an early grade, and
- More attention to the meaning of the equal sign as a description of a relationship or equivalence than as an instruction for getting an answer.

Students who do not develop these focuses will likely struggle more in algebraic situations than those who do. These concepts are all addressed in the CCSSM to build the likelihood of developing success. They are also specifically addressed in this resource in a number of the suggestions and questions provided.

There are many other issues, too, that interfere with success when students are coming to grips with algebraic situations. Some of these issues are rooted in the nature of algebra, whereas others result from missing prerequisite knowledge.

Algebra is abstract from the point of view that it is about generalizations and not specifics. Knowing that $3 \times 4 = 12$, and so does 6×2, is specific. Realizing that, when any two numbers are multiplied, the first can be doubled and the second halved without changing the product is a generalization. Many teachers focus on specifics, and many students do not get past this stage. The CCSSM suggest that teachers encourage generalization.

Students who approach problems in an unsystematic way will have more difficulty than students who are systematic in arriving at a generalization. Students who are scattered in their thinking simply do not recognize the patterns from which they might generalize. Teachers need to help students see the value of organization in detecting relationships.

Algebra requires more abstract thinking than does much work with numbers. To efficiently figure out how to graph, for example, $y = 3x - 2$ requires an understanding of the role of the coefficient of x and the constant in a linear equation. To go from tables of values to appropriate equations requires an ability to observe patterns, make sense of them, and then generalize. This type of abstract thinking requires careful development on the part of a teacher; it is not automatic for many students.

Another important prerequisite to success in algebra is a thorough understanding of addition, subtraction, multiplication, and division. To use an equation to model a problem such as "If I have 20 times as many stamps as Rachel, and I have 420 stamps, how many does Rachel have?" the student requires a deep understanding of what multiplication (or division) means, when it applies, and how to translate between natural language and algebra. In this case, a student without that knowledge might easily just multiply 20×420, seeing both of those numbers and the phrase "times as many" in the question, rather than realizing that the equation is actually $20r = 420$, which makes the question essentially a division problem. Teachers must ensure that students meet and model problems involving all sorts of meanings of operations and experience many opportunities to translate between natural language and algebra.

Algebraic reasoning often requires deduction, that is, considering how knowing one piece of information leads to another. Students without practice in this habit of mind struggle in algebra. For example, students have to understand why, if they know that $x + y = 20$, they also implicitly know that $2x + 2y = 40$, why x must be an integer if y is, and why, if y is a negative integer, then x must be a positive integer. Teachers can facilitate this habit of mind by regularly asking questions that require students to deduce.

Even relatively early work in algebra also requires some reasonable level of comfort with proportional reasoning. Thinking of $3x$ as 3 of the unit x, or of $3x + 2$ as just about the same as $3x$ for large values of x, are examples of thinking proportionally. This ability is fundamental to making sense of even simple algebraic expressions. The literature indicates that many students lack even basic proportional reasoning (Dole, 2010). Development of proportional reasoning is aided by careful teacher attention to it while teaching number, algebra, and measurement.

Yet another reason for difficulties in algebra is students' lack of understanding of the meaning of an equal sign, a critical part of algebraic thinking and a point very specifically addressed in the CCSSM. Many students think of the equal sign as a signal to perform some calculation, rather than seeing it as a way to describe two equivalent expressions or a balance. So, those students, when confronted with the equation $400 \div 2 = \square \times 5$, will assume that $\square = 200$, the answer to $400 \div 2$, rather than 40, the value that would make the two sides of the equation equal. As well, those students are totally confused by an equation like $3x + 2 = 2x + 6$, since they are looking for an answer (i.e., a number) on the right-hand side (Carpenter, Franke, & Levi, 2003; Knuth, Stephens, McNeil, & Alibali, 2006).

Students might also be confused when variables are used in different ways. For example, when a student sees $3 + k = 8$, she or he is usually expected to determine the single unknown value that makes the equation true. However, this is not the case when the student sees any of the following:

- The expression $3 + x$, which describes an infinite set of numbers;
- The function $f(x) = x + 3$, which also describes an infinite set of inputs/outputs; or
- The equation $3 + x = (5 - x) + (2x - 2)$, which is true for any value of x, not just one, since this is a statement of equivalence.

Teachers need to point out these different uses of a variable.

Hallagan (2006) points out that variables make some students so uncomfortable they often do not know how to handle them when they are included in an answer to a question, for example, a question such as "Describe an algebraic expression which means three more than a number." They believe answers should be numbers. Perhaps this is why Booth (1998) indicated that students are less comfortable with algebraic expressions than with equations; with an equation, there is at least something to do. This phenomenon means that a teacher needs to spend extra time on expressions, making the meaning of expressions clear to students. Many suggestions for focusing on expressions are provided in this resource.

Additional obstacles to success in algebra are related to missing or faulty prerequisite knowledge in students. Often this missing knowledge is a solid number sense and/or comfort with operations involving particular types of numbers. For example, solving the equation $\frac{3}{4}x = \frac{5}{8}$ requires competence with multiplication and/or division of fractions. Adding $3n$ to $(-4n)$ requires competence with addition of integers. Solving $3x - 2 = 4(x + 3)$ requires competence with order of operations. Recognizing the difference between $2 - 3x$ and $3x - 2$, or between $4(2x - 3)$ and $8x - 3$, requires an understanding of properties of numbers. Teachers need to be realistic when selecting the algebraic situations they use with students in terms of the prerequisite knowledge possessed by the students.

At the middle school level, another problem for students in understanding algebra could be lack of comfort with graphing, an important aspect of an algebra program once students begin to explore relationships between two variables. Teachers must provide students with experience in analyzing graphs and not just in creating them.

Specific Types of Algebra Errors Students Make

There are many well-documented specific errors that students make that get in the way of their success in algebra. Each of these errors is usually based on a faulty understanding of the equal sign, an incomplete understanding of what variables represent, or an inappropriate generalization of certain arithmetic ideas. Teachers aware of these specific errors can be sure to bring them to students' attention.

For example, Asquith, Stephens, Knuth, and Alibali (2007) point out that many students believe that $n + 6$ is more than $3n$, most likely because they simply think about 6 being more than 3. Falle (2007) notes that many students would interpret, for example, $3x + 5$ as $8x$ or $2(x + 5)$ as $10x$, also inappropriate generalizations of arithmetic. Teachers can make a point of having students consider such examples to illustrate appropriate reasoning.

Students are sometimes uncomfortable with notation or conventions. For example, some students do not realize that $3x$ means 3 multiplied by x, or do not understand what $f(x)$ means (Arcavi, 1994), even though they know how to deal with these ideas once they get past the notation issues. Teachers can talk much more specifically about such conventions and should not assume that students will understand after being told only once.

Christou, Vosniadou, and Vamvakoussi (2007) point out other specific errors, which include the following:

* Substituting 2 for a in $3a$ and coming up with the number 32;
* Interpreting $12m$ as 12 meters instead of as 12 times as much as the number m;
* Assuming that the letter j must be worth 10 since j is the 10th letter in the alphabet;
* Believing that to represent an amount such as hours, it is essential to use the letter h;
* Assuming that x is positive and that $-x$ is negative, even though this may not be the case;
* Assuming that in an expression such as $3x + 5$, x has to be a whole number since the expression itself involves only whole numbers;
* Believing that it is impossible for $a + b$ to be equal to $a + c$ since the letters are different, ignoring the fact that the values could be equal.

All of these misunderstandings show an underlying lack of comprehension of what variables are. Teachers can watch for these problems and address them when they arise or can illustrate the relevant concepts even in advance of a student exhibiting these misunderstandings.

Norton and Irvin (2007) point out even more errors. These include

* Rewriting $3x + 3 = 15$ as $3x = 15$, or $x - 2 = 2x + 3$ as $x = 2x + 3$, simply ignoring the 3 or -2;

- Being able to rename $3(a + b)$ as $3a + 3b$, but not $b(3 + a)$ as $3b + ab$;
- Adding 10 to h by writing $h10$ or subtracting 1 from y by writing $1y$.

These, too, show a lack of understanding of either what variables actually are or what an equation means.

Linchevski and Livneh (1999) note that students often have difficulty with subtraction and negative number issues. Many, for example, interpret $4 + n - 2 + 5$ as $4 + n - 7$, attaching the $-$ sign to the 5 as well as the 2. Perhaps this is not surprising when one considers that when children do the subtraction $431 - 112$ they are expected to apply the $-$ to the 100 as well as to the 10 and the 2 in 112. A teacher might have students look specifically at the difference between $4 + n - 2 + 5$ and $4 + n - 2 - 5$.

Arcavi (1994) describes somewhat more fundamental specific errors, which he refers to as a lack of symbol sense. For example, he notes that a student lacks symbol sense when he or she fails to notice that it is impossible to determine a value to solve $\frac{2x+3}{4x+6} = 2$ by realizing that the left-hand side is another form of the fraction $\frac{1}{2}$ unless $x = -\frac{3}{2}$, when the expression is not even defined, and $\frac{1}{2}$ cannot be equal to 2, but instead must mechanically work through the expression trying to figure it out.

Arcavi (1994) also describes the very famous incorrect equation that students write to represent the relationship that there is a professor for every six students. Instead of writing $s = 6p$, which indicates that the number of students is 6 times the number of professors, which is correct, many students write $6s = p$, translating the words directly into an untrue equation; writing $6s = p$ is wrong because that number sentence says that the number of professors is six times the number of students. This type of response, again, shows a lack of understanding of what a variable actually represents.

Similarly, MacGregor and Stacey (1993) point out that many students would write the equation $s + 8 = r$ to indicate that s is 8 more than r, rather than the correct equation $r + 8 = s$. These researchers attribute such errors to associating the 6 times or the 8 more with the variable that is greater, instead of the variable worth less, as is correct.

Asquith et al. (2007) offer another example of lack of symbol sense. They point out that many students decide whether two expressions are equivalent or not by substituting a few values to see if the results are equal and not by analyzing why the results have to be equal. For example, to decide if $3 - x = (4 + x) - (2x + 1)$, students lacking symbol sense might note that if $x = 0$, $3 = 4 - 1$; if $x = 1$, $2 = 5 - 3$; and if $x = 2$, $1 = 6 - 5$. Based on these three true statements, they conclude the expressions are equivalent. But, ideally, students should be able to interpret the symbols to see why the results had to be equal. In fact, students could draw incorrect conclusions sometimes by assuming that if the values of two expressions are equal a few times that the two expressions are always equal. This issue is addressed in suggestions made in this resource.

Addressing Student Struggles

All of the suggestions in this volume are based on a substantial literature about algebra teaching and learning that has come to recognize that instruction can make a major difference in student success with algebra concepts. Although some of the needed improvements are already reflected in the CCSSM, the delivery of these ideas through appropriate instruction and in an appropriate learning environment is a crucial element in student understanding. I believe strongly that the approaches emphasized in this resource will help support student understanding and minimize misconceptions.

FOCUSING ON THE CCSSM STANDARDS FOR MATHEMATICAL PRACTICE

The CCSSM Standards for Mathematical Practice derive from the processes of the National Council of Teachers of Mathematics (NCTM, 2000) and the strands of mathematical proficiency from *Adding It Up* (National Research Council, 2001). The standards for mathematical practice describe the mathematical environment in which it is intended that the CCSSM are learned. These standards for mathematical practice are meant to influence the instructional stance that teachers take when presenting tasks to help students grasp the content standards. The standards for mathematical practice are addressed in this resource both in the underlying ideas presented for each topic and in the types of Good Questions suggested.

Listed below are just a few examples of attention to each standard for mathematical practice in this resource.

1. ***Make sense of problems and persevere in solving them.*** Throughout the grades, many opportunities are suggested for students to use algebraic equations to represent real-life problems. It is important not only for students to be able to do this but also for them to see the value in doing so. A few very specific examples appear in the section for Grade 3, on page 24, where students represent and solve a problem relating the number of students who could be seated at a given number of tables; in the section for Grade 6, on page 85, where students create situations to match given equations; and in the section for Grade 8, on page 129, where different types of situations calling for solving two equations in two variables are described.

   The issue of perseverance cannot be dealt with directly in this resource, but is critical for teachers to encourage and support perseverance in the classroom.

2. ***Reason abstractly and quantitatively.*** Reasoning is at the heart of mathematics. Therefore, this resource provides a wealth of examples that focus on helping stu-

dents reason. A few representatives are listed here. One is found in the section for Grade 2, on page 24, where students use equations to determine whether numbers are even or odd, and one in the section for Grade 4, on page 47, where students estimate solutions to equations. Two more examples are found in the section for Grade 7, on page 106, where students solve simple inequalities and make sense of why there is an infinite number of solutions, and in the section for Grade 8, on page 115, where students make sense of how the slope of a graph relates to a unit rate description of a situation.

3. ***Construct viable arguments and critique the reasoning of others.*** Because this resource focuses on making sense of algebra, teachers are frequently encouraged to set up situations where students can make arguments as to why things happen the way they do. One example occurs in the section for Grade 1, on page 17, where students think about how actions on a physical balance match numerical situations. Another is in the section for Grade 6, on page 78, where students must create an algebraic expression that includes certain words in its natural language translation, and a third is in the section for Grade 8, on page 123, where students estimate solutions to equations, even equations involving fractions.

4. ***Model with mathematics.*** This volume includes a number of instances where algebra is used to model real-world situations. One example appears in the Grade 4 section, on page 45, where students choose appropriate equations and models for a situation. Another is in the Grade 5 section, on page 59, where students also use equations to model problems. A third example is found in the section for Grade 8, on page 120, where students model real-life relationships using a linear equation.

5. ***Use appropriate tools strategically.*** Because of the emphasis in this resource on understanding the math, there are many examples that describe the use of appropriate tools strategically. One example is in the Kindergarten section, on page 11, and another is in the Grade 1 section, on page 16, where students use a balance or Cuisenaire rods to model an equation. Discussion of the value of using the 100-chart to solve simple addition and subtraction equations appears in the section for Grade 2, on page 25.

Even in the higher grades, manipulatives and other tools are useful. In the section for Grade 6, on page 80, there is a description of the use of algebra tiles to create equivalent algebraic expressions. In the section for Grade 7, on page 104, a useful pictorial model for solving linear equations is described.

6. ***Attend to precision.*** Precision is sometimes an issue in algebra in terms of appropriate use of conventions. In the section for Grade 3, on page 30, there is a discussion of the difficulties students face with the convention used to describe division.

In the section for Grade 6, on page 74, the need for precise attention to order of operations when evaluating algebraic expressions is discussed. In the section for Grade 8, on page 154, an implicit issue of precision related to using the line of best fit is examined.

7. *Look for and make use of structure.* Mathematics is built on structure, and this volume offers many examples where structure is used to draw conclusions when studying algebra. One example is discussed in the Grade 4 section, on page 50, where students consider use of the structure of patterns to draw conclusions about their elements. Another example occurs in the Grade 5 section, on page 59, where students explore how the structure of math ensures that there are always many equations that represent a given situation. Another is in the Grade 6 section, on page 79, where students use properties of arithmetic and algebra to generate equivalent expressions.

8. *Look for and express regularity in repeated reasoning.* This standard for mathematical practice is visible in a number of situations in this resource. One is in the Grade 3 section, on page 35, where students explore addition table patterns to create generalizations. Another appears in the Grade 5 section, on page 57, where students use repeated reasoning to relate terms of two different patterns. A third is in the Grade 6 section, on page 88, where students explore the regularity in tables of values to help them understand mathematical functions.

FOCUSING ON THE CCSSM STANDARDS FOR MATHEMATICAL CONTENT

This resource is organized around the specifics of the CCSSM content standards related to instruction about algebra. Most of the specifics are listed under Operations and Algebraic Thinking, Expressions and Equations, and Functions, but some of these specifics are also found in other domains, for example, Number and Operations—Fractions, Measurement and Data, Geometry, and Statistics and Probability.

SUMMARY

Because of long-documented student struggles with algebraic thinking and particularly in light of the new Common Core State Standards for Mathematics, particularly the Standards for Mathematical Practice, it is essential for teachers to have an opportunity to deconstruct their own understanding of algebra to set the stage for enabling them to instill deeper understanding in their students.

The next sections of this resource attempt to make that easier for teachers by digging deeply into the underlying ideas that inform the standards.

KINDERGARTEN

Using Equations to Describe Addition and Subtraction

Operations and Algebraic Thinking	CCSSM K.OA

Understand addition as putting together and adding to,
and understand subtraction as taking apart and taking from.

3. Decompose numbers less than or equal to 10 into pairs in more than one way, e.g., by using objects or drawings, and record each decomposition by a drawing or equation (e.g., 5 = 2 + 3 and 5 = 4 + 1).

4. For any number from 1 to 9, find the number that makes 10 when added to the given number, e.g., by using objects or drawings, and record the answer with a drawing or equation.

IMPORTANT UNDERLYING IDEAS

> *Equations describing a balance.* An equation is a way to describe the same quantity in two different ways. Visually, it can be thought of as a balance, since neither of the two representations is worth more, or less, than the other.

For example, the equation 4 = 3 + 1 can be represented by showing how a quantity of 4 balances groups of 3 and 1 put together. In the left picture below, the balance is a balance of weight; the 4 white cubes weigh the same as 3 gray cubes and 1 dark cube. The right picture represents a balance of length; the 4 white cubes are the same length as 3 gray cubes attached to 1 dark cube.

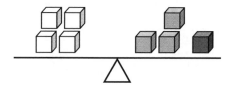

At the Kindergarten level, equations representing decomposition typically show a single number on the left being decomposed into parts, which appear on the right side of the equation, for example, $7 = 3 + 4$ rather than $3 + 4 = 7$, although clearly both equations are correct. Equations at this level typically show addition signs, but not subtraction signs, since the focus is on decomposition.

> **Equations describing a relationship.** As students work with decompositions of numbers and the related equations, they should begin to notice the sizes of the decomposed parts. For example, if 10 is decomposed, it could be decomposed into a large number and a small number (e.g., 9 and 1 or 8 and 2) or into two mid-sized numbers (e.g., $4 + 6$ or $5 + 5$).

Decompositions of 10 are particularly important in students' number development. Noticing that if one number is large, the other is small, is an example of the mathematical practice standards of looking for and making use of structure, of reasoning abstractly and quantitatively, and of looking for and expressing regularity in repeated reasoning.

> **Reading equations.** Students benefit by reading equations and having equations read to them in meaningful ways. Although we can read $5 = 2 + 3$ as "5 equals 2 plus 3," there might be value in reading it as "5 can be separated into a 2 and a 3." The latter phrasing carries more meaning for students.

Good Questions to Ask

- Provide a pan balance and linking (snap) cubes. Ask students to use the balance to model the equation $10 = 6 + 4$. Then ask them to move cubes to demonstrate a different way to show 10. [**Answer:** The student might put 10 cubes on one side of a balance and group 6 cubes and 4 cubes on the other side. All cubes must be the same size. Then the student might move 1 cube out of the group of 6 cubes to join the group of 4 cubes and indicate how or why this shows $10 = 5 + 5$.]
- Ask students: I need 10 cubes, but I don't have that many yet. If I only need a few more to have 10, how many might I have now? How many more would I need? What equation would I write? [**Answer:** Students are likely to suggest they have 8 or 9 cubes and need 2 or 1 more, writing $10 = 8 + 2$ or $10 = 9 + 1$. But if a student says he or she has 5 cubes to begin because the additional 5 needed is only a few, that is not really incorrect.]
- Ask students: Do you think there are more ways to write equations to show how you can separate a set of 8 cubes into two groups or to show how you can separate a set of 5 cubes into two groups? Why? [**Answer:** There are more combinations for 8 than for 5. There are combinations of $7 + 1$ and $6 + 2$ and $5 + 3$ and $4 + 4$ for 8, but only $4 + 1$ and $3 + 2$ for 5. (Note, by the way, that even though

this is true for whole numbers, it is not true later on, once integers, fractions, and decimals are allowed.)]

* Ask students: You break up a group of 9 cubes into two piles and write $9 = \square + ?$ to show what you did. If the first number is really small, what do you know about the second one? [***Answer:*** The second one is only a little less than 9, or maybe it is 9 if the first number is 0.]

* On a pan balance, place 10 cubes on one side and 3 cubes of one color and 7 of another on the other side. Ask students what equation this shows. [***Answer:*** $10 = 3 + 7$.]

Summary

By the end of Kindergarten, students should be familiar with the use of number equations to describe relationships between numbers based on addition. The metaphor of an equation as a balance is an important start for students' algebraic development.

GRADE 1

Using Equations to Describe Addition and Subtraction

Operations and Algebraic Thinking	CCSSM 1.OA

Represent and solve problems involving addition and subtraction.

1. Use addition and subtraction within 20 to solve word problems involving situations of adding to, taking from, putting together, taking apart, and comparing, with unknowns in all positions, e.g., by using objects, drawings, and equations with a symbol for the unknown number to represent the problem.

2. Solve word problems that call for addition of three whole numbers whose sum is less than or equal to 20, e.g., by using objects, drawings, and equations with a symbol for the unknown number to represent the problem.

Understand and apply properties of operations and the relationship between addition and subtraction.

3. Apply properties of operations as strategies to add and subtract. *Examples:* If $8 + 3 = 11$ is known, then $3 + 8 = 11$ is also known. (*Commutative property of addition.*) To add $2 + 6 + 4$, the second two numbers can be added to make a ten, so $2 + 6 + 4 = 2 + 10 = 12$. (*Associative property of addition.*)

4. Understand subtraction as an unknown-addend problem. For example, subtract $10 - 8$ by finding the number that makes 10 when added to 8.

Work with addition and subtraction equations.

7. Understand the meaning of the equal sign, and determine if equations involving addition and subtraction are true or false. For example, which of the following equations are true and which are false? $6 = 6$, $7 = 8 - 1$, $5 + 2 = 2 + 5$, $4 + 1 = 5 + 2$.

8. Determine the unknown whole number in an addition or subtraction equation relating three whole numbers. For example, determine the unknown number that makes the equation true in each of the equations $8 + ? = 11$, $5 = \square - 3$, $6 + 6 = \square$.

IMPORTANT UNDERLYING IDEAS

> *An equation as a balance.* Rather than thinking of an equation like $5 + 3 = \square$ only as a way to describe the answer when 5 is added to 3, students should be encouraged to think of an equation as a statement that describes the same amount in two different ways, one on one side of the equal sign and one on the other. Modeling an equation as a balance is particularly useful in preparing students for later grades when they will create a new equation from an existing one by either adding or subtracting the same amount on both sides. The concept of a balance supports the validity of these actions.

In 1st grade, equations typically involve either addition or subtraction signs, and there might be an operation sign on each side of the equal sign. This highlights the importance of thinking of the two sides of the equation as naming the same number. Otherwise, students might look at, for example, $4 + 3 = 5 + 2$ and think it should have read $4 + 3 = 7 + 2$ because they think of 7 as the "answer" when adding $4 + 3$.

To model an equation like $4 + 3 = 5 + 2$, students might put groups of 4 and 3 cubes on one side of a pan balance and groups of 5 and 2 cubes on the other side to see if they balance.

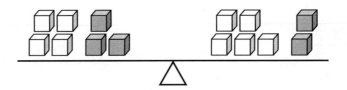

Students might also look at a length "balance" by using Cuisenaire rods and seeing that a train made up of a 4-rod and a 3-rod matches, in length, a train made up of a 5-rod and a 2-rod.

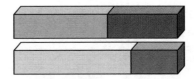

In particular, students should have opportunities to consider models for equations that illustrate the commutative and associative principles of addition. Examples would be $8 + 3 = 3 + 8$ or $4 + 8 = 2 + 10$ (another way of saying that $(2 + 2) + 8 = 2 + (2 + 8)$), where the same amount is removed from one addend and is added to the other. The Cuisenaire rod model is an excellent way to make sense of both of these equations, as shown on the next page. In the first instance, the rod pair can be viewed from the front as 8 + 3, but from the rear as 3 + 8. In the second instance, it is important to line up two pairs of rods end-to-end.

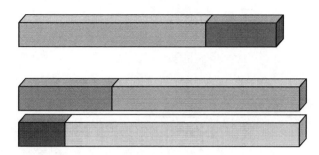

Algebraic thinking is involved as students realize why these statements are true for any numbers at all. Generalization is foundational to algebra. Students can see in the first model that turning the colors around does not change the total length: the total length has nothing to do with the *order* of the particular colors. Similarly, in the second model, they see that if two rods combine to make a particular length and one of those rods is a certain amount shorter than one of the rods in another pair of the same total length, that amount must be added to the "partner" of the shorter rod in order to keep the lengths of the two pairs equal. Again, the specific values are irrelevant.

Students could also consider how to model a subtraction equation with either a balance or rods. For example, for 5 = 7 – 2, students might put 5 cubes on one side of the balance and 7 on the other. The imbalance makes it easy to see the need to take away 2 from the 7 side to achieve balance.

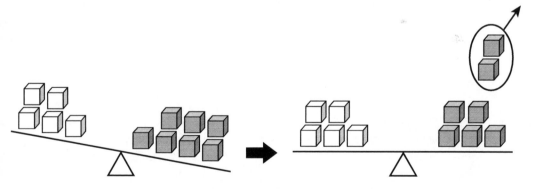

With Cuisenaire rods, students can think of 7 – 2 as how much of a 7-rod is left if 2 is "used up," or, in other words, how much longer a 7-rod is than a 2-rod.

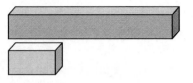

Since a 5-rod fills the missing space, 7 – 2 = 5.

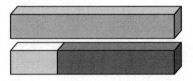

Some students will see an equation like 7 – 2 = 5 and think, "If I count back 2 spaces from 7 on a number line, I get to 5, so 7 – 2 is 5."

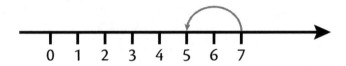

It is important for students to be aware that an equation that is *not* true might be presented to them for the purpose of verifying its truth. This can be tricky for students if we overemphasize the idea that an equation is true, as we generally do when students are looking for a missing value, where we want the equation to be true.

> *An equation as describing a relationship.* Students might be encouraged to look at relationships between numbers as described in equations. For example, when they consider the equation 6 = 4 + 2 and recognize its truth, they might note that both 4 and 2 are less than 6, since the two numbers are put together to make 6. On the other hand, when considering the equation 8 = 10 – 2, students might note that 10 is more than 8 since part of the 10 is taken away to get to the 8, or they might see it as a way of saying that 10 is 2 more than 8.

With equations with operations on both sides, for example, 5 + 3 = 6 + 2, students might note that since the 6 is more than the 5, the number added to the 6 has to be less than the number added to the 5 in order for the values on the two sides to be equal. This is an example of the mathematical practice standard of reasoning abstractly and quantitatively.

> *An equation as modeling a problem.* Most of the equations students use at this level should describe real-life situations. For example, students might relate a

problem involving combining 3 children with 4 more children to the equation $3 + 4 = \square$.

Subtraction equations are more complex for students because situations that sound quite different might be modeled with the same equation. For example, the equation $5 - 2 = \square$ can represent any of these three problems:

- If there were 5 children in the room and 2 left, how many would remain in the room?
- How much older is Abbie than Liam if Abbie is 5 years old and Liam is 2?
- If I have 2 stickers, how many more do I need to have 5 stickers?

Notice, too, that it might make sense to model the last two problems with the equation $2 + \square = 5$.

> *Meaning of an unknown.* Grade 1 is the first grade where variables are intro-duced. Rather than using letters as variables, other symbols—frames, shapes, blanks, question marks, or some combination thereof—are used. Students need to learn that the goal is to figure out what the missing value is. There is no need to call the missing value a "variable," even though it is, although there is nothing wrong with using that term.

It is important that the missing value appear in different positions in the equa-tion, for example, $\square + 4 = 6$, $2 + \square = 6$, $2 + 4 = \square$, $8 - 2 = \square$, $8 - \square = 2$. Students typically struggle least with equations in the forms $a + b = \square$ or $a - b = \square$, more with equations of the form $a + \square = c$ or $a - \square = c$, and most with equations of the form $\square + b = c$ or $\square - b = c$. This might be because finding the result when all the information is given is what students are most accustomed to; they are less accus-tomed to figuring out what action took place to change one number to another and even less familiar with situations where they do not know how they started but have to figure out where they ended based on a described change.

When equations have operation signs on both sides, it is critical that students think of the equal sign as a description of a balance. For example, some students solve an equation like $5 + 8 = \square + 3$ by indicating that $\square$ is worth 13, since they see the equal sign as asking for an answer instead of indicating a balance.

When an equation involves the addition of three numbers, it might be easier for students if the unknown is alone on one side of the equal sign, either on the left or on the right.

> *Reading equations.* Students benefit by reading equations or having equations read to them in meaningful ways. Although we can read $7 = 10 - 3$ as "7 equals 10 minus 3," there might be value in reading this equation as "7 is what is left after 3 is taken away from 10." The latter phrasing carries more meaning for students.

Similarly, reading an equation with an unknown should be done meaningfully. We might read, for example, 7 + 4 = ☐ as "What would balance a group of 7 put together with a group of 4 on the pan balance?" We might read 8 – ☐ = 2 as "What can I take away from 8 to be left with 2?" or "What must I add to 2 to get 8?" rather than as "8 minus what equals 2?"

Good Questions to Ask

* Ask students to complete the other side of this equation two ways, first to make it true and then to make it false: 6 + 3 = ☐ [**Answer:** The equation is true only if the question mark is replaced by 9; any other value makes it false.]
* Ask students whether each of these equations is true or not, and whether it is easy to tell or not, and why:

$$9 + 1 = 8 + 1$$
$$8 + 5 = 6 + 7$$
$$5 + 5 = 6 + 4$$
$$1 + 1 = 2$$
$$3 = 5 + 2$$
$$8 - 1 = 9$$
$$7 - 1 = 6$$

[**Answer:** Different opinions are possible, but many students find the first one easy since the next number after 9, which is what you get when you add 1, cannot be the same as the next number after 8. Some students might notice, in 8 + 5 = 6 + 7, that 2 of the 8 is just moved over to increase the 5 to 7, so the results are the same, but many will find it more difficult to decide whether the second equation is true than the first equation. Some students will realize, in the equation 5 + 5 = 6 + 4, that 1 is moved from the second 5 to increase the first 5, so the equation is true, but others will likely not see that; they might, however, find the equation easy to verify since both sides add to 10, a familiar sum for many students. In the next equation, most students know that 1 + 1 is 2 and will quickly recognize that the equation 1 + 1 = 2 is true. Some students will struggle with 3 = 5 + 2 because they will see the familiar numbers 3, 2, and 5 and will not think about the fact that the operations are wrongly placed. The same issue will arise with 8 – 1 = 9. Many, but not all, students will find the equation 7 – 1 = 6 easy since they can just count back one number from 7.]
* Provide either Cuisenaire rods or a pan balance and linking (snap) cubes and ask students to choose an equation to model. Students who are ready should be encouraged to consider equations with operation signs on both sides. [**Answer:** There are many choices. Some examples are 4 + 3 = 7 or 4 + 2 = 5 + 1 or 8 – 2 = 6 or 9 – 1 = 7 + 1.]

- Provide a selection of equations with missing values, such as the ones below. Ask students to explain how they know the missing value is less than 5 each time.

$$7 + \square = 10$$
$$8 = 4 + \square$$
$$9 - 6 = \square$$
$$10 - \square = 8$$

[**Answer:** Many students will simply solve the equation to see if the result is less than 5. Others will use the mathematical practice standard of reasoning abstractly and quantitatively. For example, they might say, in the first case, that $7 + 5 = 12$ and since you only want 10, 5 is too much. Or they might say, for the last one, if you take away 5, you have 5 left. But you want 8 left, you have to take away less.]

- Provide a variety of addition and subtraction stories and ask students to model them with equations.
- Provide a simple equation such as $8 - 6 = \square$ and ask students to tell a story that goes with the equation.

Summary

By the end of Grade 1, students should be thinking of an equation as a balance. The idea of balance may be viewed as just two ways of saying the same amount and/or as a physical balance of mass or length. Students should be able to interpret simple addition and subtraction equations with or without unknowns and, ideally, should be able to model those equations in some ways. Equations with unknowns should include each of these types: $a + b = \square$, $a + \square = c$, $\square + b = c$, $a - b = \square$, $a - \square = c$, and $\square - b = c$.

Using Equations to Represent Problems and Relationships

Operations and Algebraic Thinking	CCSSM 2.OA
Represent and solve problems involving addition and subtraction.	

1. Use addition and subtraction within 100 to solve one- and two-step word problems involving situations of adding to, taking from, putting together, taking apart, and comparing, with unknowns in all positions, e.g., by using drawings and equations with a symbol for the unknown number to represent the problem.

Work with equal groups of objects to gain foundations for multiplication.

3. Determine whether a group of objects (up to 20) has an odd or even number of members, e.g., by pairing objects or counting them by 2s; write an equation to express an even number as a sum of two equal addends.
4. Use addition to find the total number of objects arranged in rectangular arrays with up to 5 rows and up to 5 columns; write an equation to express the total as a sum of equal addends.

IMPORTANT UNDERLYING IDEAS

➢ *Flexibility in equations used.* Although students in earlier grades will have met equations, there is more expectation of using equations to represent problems in Grade 2 than there was previously. The problems students model at this level could involve addition or subtraction or both. A useful tool for modeling either addition or subtraction situations is shown below.

Whole	
Part	Part

Either the whole is missing (an addition situation) or one part is missing (a subtraction situation). Using a representation like this involves the mathematical practice standard of using appropriate tools strategically; modeling problems with equations involves using the practice standard of modeling.

It is important that students realize that there are always choices in how to represent a problem with an equation. For example, for a problem such as "There were 23 students in one class and 28 in another. How many were there altogether?" the equation might be $23 + 28 = \square$ or $28 + 23 = \square$.

For a problem such as "One table was 60" long and another was 42" long. How much longer was the longer table?" the equation might be $60 - 42 = \square$ or $42 + \square = 60$ or $60 - \square = 42$. It is for this reason that it is particularly important that students not be asked to identify whether a problem is an addition problem or a subtraction problem. Any subtraction equation can also be written as an addition equation.

It is valuable to use problems that lead to equations where the missing number appears in different positions in the equation, for example, $\square + 42 = 65$, $23 + \square = 64$, $23 + 47 = \square$, $82 - 24 = \square$, $84 - \square = 26$, and $\square - 35 = 34$.

Students also need experiences to show them that the same equation can model very different situations. For example, the equation $31 - \square = 17$ could model a problem such as "It is the 17th of the month. How many more days until the end of the month?" Or it could model "I had \$31. I spent some money and there was \$17 left. How much did I spend?"

> **Reading equations.** Students benefit by reading equations or having equations read to them in meaningful ways. Although we can read $\square = 30 - 3$ as "What equals 30 minus 3?" there might be value in reading this equation as "How much more is 30 than 3?" or "How much is left if 3 is removed from 30?" or "How much must I add to 3 to get up to 30?"

> **The concept of "even."** When a student is asked to show that a number is even by writing an appropriate equation, he or she needs to realize that there are two possibilities. Often, a student will write a number added to itself, for example, 42 is even since $42 = 21 + 21$, the sum of two identical numbers. Because the first 21 matches the second 21, the parts of 42 are paired up, which is what evenness is all about. However, if a student chooses to write $42 = 2 + 2 + 2 + 2 + \ldots + 2 + 2$ (21 times), this is another legitimate way to show that the number 42 is even, since, again, the number is broken up into matching pairs. In general, a whole number is even if it is the sum of many 2s or the sum of two of the same whole number.

> **The 100-chart as a tool for solving equations.** It is assumed that 2nd-grade students will still often use concrete materials and/or diagrams to solve an equation, although some will be able to work more symbolically.

A useful tool might be a 100-chart. To solve an equation like 42 + □ = 60, students might start at 42 and see how many spaces they must move to get to 60.

1	2	3	4	5	6	7	8	9	10
11	12	13	14	15	16	17	18	19	20
21	22	23	24	25	26	27	28	29	30
31	32	33	34	35	36	37	38	39	40
41	42	43	44	45	46	47	48	49	50
51	52	53	54	55	56	57	58	59	60
61	62	63	64	65	66	67	68	69	70
71	72	73	74	75	76	77	78	79	80
81	82	83	84	85	86	87	88	89	90
91	92	93	94	95	96	97	98	99	100

To solve an equation like 28 + 42 = □, students could start at 28, add 42 by adding 4 tens (going down 4 rows) and 2 more, and look for the landing spot.

1	2	3	4	5	6	7	8	9	10
11	12	13	14	15	16	17	18	19	20
21	22	23	24	25	26	27	28	29	30
31	32	33	34	35	36	37	38▾	39	40
41	42	43	44	45	46	47	48▾	49	50
51	52	53	54	55	56	57	58▾	59	60
61	62	63	64	65	66	67	68▾	69	70
71	72	73	74	75	76	77	78	79	80
81	82	83	84	85	86	87	88	89	90
91	92	93	94	95	96	97	98	99	100

Students might also use other tools, such as base-ten blocks or ten-frames and counters, to solve these problems. For example, to solve 28 + 42 with base-ten blocks, the student might represent each amount and combine 10-blocks and 1-blocks.

To model $28 + \square = 42$ with ten-frames and counters, students might represent 28 on ten-frames and pay attention to how many counters must be added to get to 42.

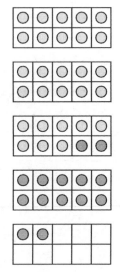

The focus, though, should be on thinking about what the equation says. For example, students should realize that the equation $90 - 24 = \square$ is asking how much more 90 is than 24, what to add to 24 to get 90, or what is left if 24 is removed from 90. Which language is used should depend on the nature of the problem—whether it is a comparison, a missing addend, or a take-away problem.

At this stage it would be inappropriate to provide rules to students for solving equations. They should be working their way to the solution by thinking about what the equation means or says.

Although standard 2.OA.1 makes a distinction between one-step and two-step problems, there is no need for students to note these distinctions so long as the teacher ensures that both types of problems are encountered.

➤ *Foundations for multiplication.* As students in higher grades develop their multiplication skills, an array is one of the suggested tools. An array makes it easy for students to see how many equal groups there are.

To prepare for application of arrays to multiplication, arrays might be introduced at the 2nd-grade level. Although students will still use addition (rather than multiplication) to describe the total number of items in the array, familiarity with arrays can be useful.

For example, to determine how the number of stars below, students would write 4 + 4 + 4 = 12.

Good Questions to Ask

* Ask students for alternate ways to write a given equation, for example, 14 + □ = 28. [**Answer:** 28 − □ = 14 or 7 + 7 + □ = 28 or . . . .]
* Provide a comparison problem and ask students to write the equation that matches it first by using an addition sign in the equation and then by using a subtraction sign in an alternate equation. An example of such a problem is "Your mom is 12 years older than her sister. If your mom is 39, how old is her sister?" [**Answer:** 12 + □ = 39 or □ + 12 = 39 or 39 − 12 = □ or 39 − □ = 12.]
* Ask students to describe two completely different-sounding problems that might be modeled by the equation 20 − 12 = □. [**Answer (examples):** I had 20 cookies and we ate 12. How many are left? **OR** My brother is 20 years old and my sister is 12 years old. How much older is my brother than my sister? **OR** I have $12 already but need more to buy a $20 game. How much more do I need?]
* Ask students to describe how they would solve the equation 37 + □ = 81. Provide any tools they might need (e.g., ten-frames and counters or base-ten blocks). [**Answer:** Some might suggest that they try adding different numbers to 37 until one works. Others might subtract 37 from 81 by using a particular strategy or algorithm. Others might count up on a 100-chart, realizing they might begin at 37 and go 5 lines down and 6 spaces back.]
* Ask students to write an equation involving numbers greater than 10 that they think would be easy to solve and then to explain why their equation is easy to solve. Explaining why an equation is easy to solve is an example of the mathematical practice standard of constructing a viable argument. Encouraging students to share their ideas with others provides an opportunity for students to critique the reasoning of others. [**Answer:** There are many possible answers, for example, 20 + □ = 40. Students might say that this equation is easy to solve since they know that 20 and 20 is 40 or they know that 2 and 2 is 4, so 20 and 20 is 40.]

• Ask students what each of these equations tells about whether the number on the left is even or odd.

$$\text{Equation 1: } 22 = 11 + 11$$
$$\text{Equation 2: } 31 = 15 + 16$$
$$\text{Equation 3: } 12 = 2 + 2 + 2 + 2 + 2 + 2$$
$$\text{Equation 4: } 15 = 2 + 2 + 2 + 2 + 2 + 2 + 2 + 1$$

[*Answer:* Equations 1 and 3 show even numbers since there are either two of the same number or lots of 2s. Equations 2 and 4 show that the numbers are odd. Equation 2 shows that 31 is odd since the fact that 15 and 16 are next to each other means it is impossible to write 31 as the sum of two of the same whole number. Equation 4 shows that 15 is odd since it is made up of a lot of 2s but then there is still a 1 left over.]

• Ask students to draw an array and use an addition sentence to describe the total number of items in the array.

Summary

By the end of Grade 2, students should show flexibility in the addition and subtraction equations they use to model problems, generally involving one-digit or two-digit numbers, and they should recognize that the same equation could model many different situations. They should use a variety of tools for solving addition and subtraction equations involving one-digit and two-digit numbers, including the 100-chart. They also get ready for multiplication by recognizing addition sentences that describe arrays or addition sentences that describe whether numbers are even or not.

GRADE 3

Using Equations to Represent Problems

Operations and Algebraic Thinking	CCSSM 3.OA

Represent and solve problems involving multiplication and division.

3. Use multiplication and division within 100 to solve word problems in situations involving equal groups, arrays, and measurement quantities, e.g., by using drawings and equations with a symbol for the unknown number to represent the problem.

4. Determine the unknown whole number in a multiplication or division equation relating three whole numbers. For example, determine the unknown number that makes the equation true in each of the equations $8 \times ? = 48$, $5 = \square \div 3$, $6 \times 6 = ?$.

Understand properties of multiplication and the relationship between multiplication and division.

5. Apply properties of operations as strategies to multiply and divide. *Examples:* If $6 \times 4 = 24$ is known, then $4 \times 6 = 24$ is also known. (*Commutative property of multiplication.*) $3 \times 5 \times 2$ can be found by $3 \times 5 = 15$, then $15 \times 2 = 30$, or by $5 \times 2 = 10$, then $3 \times 10 = 30$. (*Associative property of multiplication.*) Knowing that $8 \times 5 = 40$ and $8 \times 2 = 16$, one can find 8×7 as $8 \times (5 + 2) = (8 \times 5) + (8 \times 2) = 40 + 16 = 56$. (*Distributive property.*)

6. Understand division as an unknown-factor problem. For example, find $32 \div 8$ by finding the number that makes 32 when multiplied by 8.

Solve problems involving the four operations, and identify and explain patterns in arithmetic.

8. Solve two-step word problems using the four operations. Represent these problems using equations with a letter standing for the unknown quantity. Assess the reasonableness of answers using mental computation and estimation strategies including rounding.

IMPORTANT UNDERLYING IDEAS

> *Conventions in multiplication and division expressions.* Having already experi-
enced addition and subtraction equations, students move at this level to multiplication and division equations.

Students must become familiar with certain conventions. For example, in
North America, $b \times c$ normally means b groups of size c, rather than c groups of
size b. (This is not the standard convention in all countries.) Although students
eventually learn that the expressions $b \times c$ and $c \times b$ are interchangeable, consistency in what the expressions mean is valuable, particularly initially.

So, for example, students would be encouraged to represent the problem
"There are 3 baskets of apples with 7 apples in each basket. How many apples are
there?" with the equation $3 \times 7 = ?$. However, if a student writes $7 \times 3 = ?$, this is
not incorrect but merely inconsistent with a convention.

Because multiplication is defined on two numbers, students might wonder
about the convention for multiplying three numbers, e.g., $5 \times 2 \times 9$. They need to
learn that they can approach that problem in either of two ways: they can first
multiply 5×2 and then multiply that product by 9, or they can multiply 5 by the
product of 2 and 9. Sometimes the choice is based on convenience. For example, it
is easier mentally to multiply 5×2 and then the product by 9 than it is to multiply
5 by the product of 2 and 9. One way for a student to realize why the associative
property makes sense might be to consider a $5 \times 2 \times 9$ block and realize that
counting individual cubes making up the block could be done as 5 strips of 2×9
cubes or as 9 strips of 5×2 cubes.

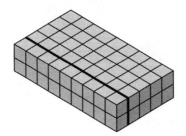 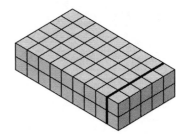

The equation $b \div c = ?$ might be interpreted as asking for the group size if
there are b items being distributed into c equal groups, but it might also be interpreted as asking for the number of groups if b items are being grouped c at a time.
In either case, the total of b items is formed into equal groups and either how
many groups or the size of each group is known.

When representing equations, many students write $3 \div 15 = ?$ when they actually mean $15 \div 3 = ?$. This becomes even more common later on, when long division is introduced and the divisor is seen to the left. Again, it is helpful to treat this
as a misunderstanding of convention rather than as a real error. Later, as students

work with fractional values, the distinction between $15 \div 3$ and $3 \div 15$ becomes even more important to clarify.

> **Flexibility in equations used.** As with the addition and subtraction situations met earlier, it is important that students realize that there are always choices in how to represent a multiplication or division problem with an equation. For example, for a problem such as "There were 15 cookies being shared equally by 5 children. How many does each get?" the equation might be $5 \times ? = 15$ or it might be $15 \div 5 = \square$ or it might be $15 \div \square = 5$.

> **Letter variables for the unknown.** At the 3rd-grade level, students are expected to begin to use letters rather than symbols such as question marks, open boxes, shapes, etc. to represent an unknown.

For some students, letters are more challenging and the transition might be slower. Students should realize that a letter really is equivalent to a question mark or an open box.

Students need to become aware that any letter they choose is acceptable, and no one letter is preferable to another. Many teachers and students advocate using a letter that helps the student remember what the value represents. For example, in the problem "There were 24 students at 4 tables. The same number of students was at each table. How many were at each table?" students might use s in the equation $24 \div 4 = s$ to represent students in the problem. Many students just pick any word in the problem to suggest a letter and might use t from table. This, again, is not incorrect, but in the end it is critical that the students understand what their answer represents—the number of students at each table, not the number of tables.

> **Using manipulatives to solve equations based on real-life problems.** At this level, it is assumed that students are allowed to use concrete materials and/or diagrams to solve an equation, although some will choose to work symbolically. Especially for multiplication and division, which are still relatively new, students should be encouraged to use materials such as counters.

In general, multiplication and division equations should come from appropriate problems involving equal groups, arrays, or measurement situations. For example, the equation $3 \times 5 = \square$ might describe the total number of items in a 3 by 5 array, the total number of items in 3 groups of 5, or the total measure of 3 units of 5 (e.g., 3 distances of 5" or the area of 3 tiles each made up of 5 squares). The equation $15 \div 3 = \square$ might describe the size of each group if 15 is separated into 3 equal groups. Or $15 \div 3 = \square$ might describe the number of groups of 3 that can be created from a total of 15 items.

Third-grade students should continue to solve addition and subtraction problems, too, although the numbers involved might be more complex than was the case in 2nd grade.

> *Using personal strategies to solve equations.* It is still too early to impose "methods" to solve equations. Students should be encouraged to use personal strategies to make sense of what the equations say. For example, for $w \times 7 = 35$ (to solve a problem asking how many weeks in 35 days), students should be thinking, "How many 7s make 35? Is it as many as 10? Is it just a few? How many make sense?" This is preferable to simply telling students to divide if they see a multiplication sign (which could lead to trouble in the equation $4 \times 3 = \square$) or to multiply if they see a division sign.

Good Questions to Ask

- Ask students for alternate ways to write a given equation, for example, $3 \times m = 24$. [*Answer:* Possibly $m \times 3 = 24$, but also $24 \div 3 = m$ or $24 \div m = 3$ or $m + m + m = 24$.]
- Provide a sharing problem and (before it is actually solved) ask students to write an equation that matches it, first by using a division sign in the equation and then by using a multiplication sign in another equation. A sample sharing problem might involve a certain number of children sharing a certain number of cookies. [*Answer (examples):* $12 \div 3 = c$ or $12 \div c = 3$ or $3 \times c = 12$.]
- Ask students how they could rewrite the multiplication equation $4 \times m = 12$ as an addition equation. Recognizing that any multiplication can be written as an addition is an example of the mathematical practice standard of looking for and expressing regularity in repeated reasoning. [*Answer:* $m + m + m + m = 12$ or $2 \times m + 2 \times m = 12$ or $3 \times m + m = 12$ or even $0 + 4 \times m = 12$.]
- Ask students to describe how they would solve the equation $37 + k = 81 + 12$. Provide any tools they might need, such as 100-charts, ten-frames and counters, or base-ten blocks. [*Answer:* Some students might use a 100-chart, start at 81, go down 1 and over 2 to land at 93, and then figure out how to start at 37 and end at 93. Some students might take 8 base-ten rods and 1 one-block, add that to 1 base-ten rod and 2 one-blocks, and then separate the total into a group of 4 rods and the rest. They could realize that the answer is the rest plus 3 ones, because the group of 4 rods (40) is 3 more than the 37 in the equation they are solving. Some students will just add $81 + 12$ to get 93 and then subtract 37 using some known strategy.]
- Tell students that someone solved a division problem and the answer was 8. Have them write a possible problem and its equation. [*Answer:* One example is a problem where 3 children share 24 books and we want to know how many each gets. The equation might be $24 \div 3 = b$.]
- Tell students that someone solved a problem involving both addition and subtraction. The answer was 24. Have them write a possible problem and its equation. [*Answer:* One example is a problem where a group of 13 children and a group of 12 children joined up. Then 1 child left and we want to know how many children remained. The equation might be $13 + 12 - 1 = c$, or $13 - 1 + 12 = c$, etc.]

Patterns in the Addition and Multiplication Tables

Operations and Algebraic Thinking	CCSSM 3.OA
Solve problems involving the four operations, and identify and explain patterns in arithmetic.	

9. Identify arithmetic patterns (including patterns in the addition table or multiplication table), and explain them using properties of operations. For example, observe that 4 times a number is always even, and explain why 4 times a number can be decomposed into two equal addends.

IMPORTANT UNDERLYING IDEAS

> *Changing order of addends in the addition table.* The commutative property of addition, one that is very useful, states that numbers can be added in any order. To see this on the addition table, students need to compare sums such as 4 + 3 to 3 + 4 and 8 + 2 to 2 + 8. Ultimately, students should see that it is the symmetry of the addition table along the diagonal that shows us this equality.

For example, in the table below, 4 + 3 and 3 + 4, as well as 8 + 2 and 2 + 8, are highlighted. In both cases, the two sums are equally distant from the diagonal reflection line.

+	0	1	2	3	4	5	6	7	8	9
0	0	1	2	3	4	5	6	7	8	9
1	1	2	3	4	5	6	7	8	9	10
2	2	3	4	5	6	7	8	9	10	11
3	3	4	5	6	7	8	9	10	11	12
4	4	5	6	7	8	9	10	11	12	13
5	5	6	7	8	9	10	11	12	13	14
6	6	7	8	9	10	11	12	13	14	15
7	7	8	9	10	11	12	13	14	15	16
8	8	9	10	11	12	13	14	15	16	17
9	9	10	11	12	13	14	15	16	17	18

It is important that students understand that the table shows that the commutative property seems to hold, but not why. Other methods focused on the meaning of addition are needed to explain why.

It is also useful for students to understand when the commutative property is useful. For example, it is easier to mentally consider $1 + 8$ by starting at 8 and moving forward 1 number (which is $8 + 1$) than by starting at 1 and counting forward 8 numbers.

> **Showing subtraction in the addition table.** Students might recognize that since, if $a + b = c$, then $c - a = b$, they could solve a subtraction problem such as $17 - 8$ by locating the sum 17 in the row for 8 and then determining the column heading, in this case, 9.

+	0	1	2	3	4	5	6	7	8	9
0	0	1	2	3	4	5	6	7	8	9
1	1	2	3	4	5	6	7	8	9	10
2	2	3	4	5	6	7	8	9	10	11
3	3	4	5	6	7	8	9	10	11	12
4	4	5	6	7	8	9	10	11	12	13
5	5	6	7	8	9	10	11	12	13	14
6	6	7	8	9	10	11	12	13	14	15
7	7	8	9	10	11	12	13	14	15	16
8	8	9	10	11	12	13	14	15	16	17
9	9	10	11	12	13	14	15	16	17	18

Students should recognize, therefore, why there is no need for a subtraction table. Addition and subtraction are so intertwined that each is embedded in the other.

> **Increasing an addend by a fixed amount in the addition table.** Students should observe that choosing any position in the table and increasing one addend by some amount (either by going down or across a certain number of rows or columns) leads to a sum that is that amount greater.

For example, at the top of the next page one can see that $5 + 5$ is 2 more than $5 + 3$ since 5 is 2 more than 3. Similarly, $4 + 8$ is 2 more than $2 + 8$ since 4 is 2 more than 2. In other words, moving 2 spaces down increases a sum by 2; moving 2 spaces to the right increases a sum by 2.

+	0	1	2	3	4	5	6	7	8	9
0	0	1	2	3	4	5	6	7	8	9
1	1	2	3	4	5	6	7	8	9	10
2	2	3	4	5	6	7	8	9	10	11
3	3	4	5	6	7	8	9	10	11	12
4	4	5	6	7	8	9	10	11	12	13
5	5	6	7	8	9	10	11	12	13	14
6	6	7	8	9	10	11	12	13	14	15
7	7	8	9	10	11	12	13	14	15	16
8	8	9	10	11	12	13	14	15	16	17
9	9	10	11	12	13	14	15	16	17	18

Increasing one addend by some selected amount and decreasing the other addend by the same amount has the effect of moving diagonally up to the right or down to the left on the addition table. Notice that these diagonals have identical values all the way up and down the diagonal, so the sums are equal. This is, in fact, a description of the associative property for addition.

For example, the sums for 7 + 5 and 4 + 8 (*notice that 7 is decreased by 3 and 5 is increased by 3*) are highlighted below.

+	0	1	2	3	4	5	6	7	8	9
0	0	1	2	3	4	5	6	7	8	9
1	1	2	3	4	5	6	7	8	9	10
2	2	3	4	5	6	7	8	9	10	11
3	3	4	5	6	7	8	9	10	11	12
4	4	5	6	7	8	9	10	11	12	13
5	5	6	7	8	9	10	11	12	13	14
6	6	7	8	9	10	11	12	13	14	15
7	7	8	9	10	11	12	13	14	15	16
8	8	9	10	11	12	13	14	15	16	17
9	9	10	11	12	13	14	15	16	17	18

➤ **Adding 0 and adding 1 in the addition table.** Students might examine the sums in the first row (or column) of the table to observe that the numbers match the row (or column) headings. This shows that adding 0 does not change a number.

Students might examine the sums in the second row (or column) and notice that the values are one greater than the row (or column) headings. This shows the effect of adding 1.

+	0	1	2	3	4	5	6	7	8	9
0	0	1	2	3	4	5	6	7	8	9
1	1	2	3	4	5	6	7	8	9	10
2	2	3	4	5	6	7	8	9	10	11
3	3	4	5	6	7	8	9	10	11	12
4	4	5	6	7	8	9	10	11	12	13
5	5	6	7	8	9	10	11	12	13	14
6	6	7	8	9	10	11	12	13	14	15
7	7	8	9	10	11	12	13	14	15	16
8	8	9	10	11	12	13	14	15	16	17
9	9	10	11	12	13	14	15	16	17	18

➤ **Order of numbers in the multiplication table.** The commutative property of multiplication states that numbers can be multiplied in any order. To see this in the multiplication table, students need to compare products such as 4×3 to 3×4 or 8×2 to 2×8. Ultimately, students should see that it is the symmetry of the multiplication table along the diagonal that shows this equivalence.

For example, in the table at the top of the next page, 4×3 and 3×4, as well as 8×2 and 2×8, are highlighted. Each product within a pair is an equal distance from the diagonal line drawn on the table. This is an example of the mathematical practice standard of looking for and expressing regularity in repeated reasoning.

×	0	1	2	3	4	5	6	7	8	9
0	0	0	0	0	0	0	0	0	0	0
1	0	1	2	3	4	5	6	7	8	9
2	0	2	4	6	8	10	12	14	16	18
3	0	3	6	9	12	15	18	21	24	27
4	0	4	8	12	16	20	24	28	32	36
5	0	5	10	15	20	25	30	35	40	45
6	0	6	12	18	24	30	36	42	48	54
7	0	7	14	21	28	35	42	49	56	63
8	0	8	16	24	33	40	48	56	64	72
9	0	9	18	27	36	45	54	63	72	81

> **Embedded division in the multiplication table.** Students might recognize that since, if $a \times b = c$, then $c \div a = b$, they could solve a division problem such as $56 \div 8$ by locating the product 56 in the row for 8 and then determining the column heading, in this case 7.

×	0	1	2	3	4	5	6	7	8	9
0	0	0	0	0	0	0	0	0	0	0
1	0	1	2	3	4	5	6	7	8	9
2	0	2	4	6	8	10	12	14	16	18
3	0	3	6	9	12	15	18	21	24	27
4	0	4	8	12	16	20	24	28	32	36
5	0	5	10	15	20	25	30	35	40	45
6	0	6	12	18	24	30	36	42	48	54
7	0	7	14	21	28	35	42	49	56	63
8	0	8	16	24	33	40	48	56	64	72
9	0	9	18	27	36	45	54	63	72	81

> **Increasing a factor by 1 in the multiplication table.** Increasing a factor by 1 results in an increase in the product, specifically an increase that is the size of the other factor. For example, 3×8 is 3 more than 3×7 since there is 1 extra in each of the 3 groups; 3×8 is 8 more than 2×8 since there is 1 extra group of 8. These

are special cases of the distributive property, that is, $a \times (b + 1) = a \times b + a$ or $(a + 1) \times b = a \times b + b$.

Students see this in the table by examining the products in any row and the row below it or in any column and the column next to it. For example, in the diagram below one sees that each value in the row for 4 is more than the value in the row for 3; the amount more is the column heading, which is the other factor. One also sees that each value in the column for 7 is more than the value in the column for 6; the amount more is the row heading, which is the other factor.

×	0	1	2	3	4	5	6	7	8	9
0	0	0	0	0	0	0	0	0	0	0
1	0	1	2	3	4	5	6	7	8	9
2	0	2	4	6	8	10	12	14	16	18
3	0	3	6	9	12	15	18	21	24	27
4	0	4	8	12	16	20	24	28	32	36
5	0	5	10	15	20	25	30	35	40	45
6	0	6	12	18	24	30	36	42	48	54
7	0	7	14	21	28	35	42	49	56	63
8	0	8	16	24	33	40	48	56	64	72
9	0	9	18	27	36	45	54	63	72	81

➢ *Adding rows or columns in the multiplication table.* Adding matching numbers in any two rows (or any two columns) results in the numbers in another row (or column). In essence, this is a description of the distributive property. For example, adding the numbers in the row for 2 with the matching numbers in the row for 3 results in the numbers that appear in the row for 5 (as shown at the top of the next page). This is because if 2 of something is added to 3 of that thing, you end up with 5 of that thing.

×	0	1	2	3	4	5	6	7	8	9
0	0	0	0	0	0	0	0	0	0	0
1	0	1	2	3	4	5	6	7	8	9
2	0	2	4	6	8	10	12	14	16	18
3	0	3	6	9	12	15	18	21	24	27
4	0	4	8	12	16	20	24	28	32	36
5	0	5	10	15	20	25	30	35	40	45
6	0	6	12	18	24	30	36	42	48	54
7	0	7	14	21	28	35	42	49	56	63
8	0	8	16	24	33	40	48	56	64	72
9	0	9	18	27	36	45	54	63	72	81

Similarly, adding products in the column for 2 to the corresponding products in the column for 3 results in the products in the column for 5 (as shown below). This is because having a number of 2s and the same number of 3s is equivalent to having that number of 5s (by combining each 2 with a 3).

×	0	1	2	3	4	5	6	7	8	9
0	0	0	0	0	0	0	0	0	0	0
1	0	1	2	3	4	5	6	7	8	9
2	0	2	4	6	8	10	12	14	16	18
3	0	3	6	9	12	15	18	21	24	27
4	0	4	8	12	16	20	24	28	32	36
5	0	5	10	15	20	25	30	35	40	45
6	0	6	12	18	24	30	36	42	48	54
7	0	7	14	21	28	35	42	49	56	63
8	0	8	16	24	33	40	48	56	64	72
9	0	9	18	27	36	45	54	63	72	81

> **Multiplying a factor in the multiplication table.** Students might notice that if the column (or row) header is doubled, so are the values of the products in that column (or row).

In the diagram below, for example, the rows for 4 and 8 are highlighted; all values in the row for 8 are double the corresponding values in the row for 4. This is because 8 groups of something is twice as much as 4 groups of that thing. Similarly, the values for the column for 6 are double the corresponding values in the column for 3. This is because a bunch of 6s can be subdivided into twice as many bunches of 3s. For example, $8 \times 5 = 2 \times (4 \times 5)$ or $7 \times 6 = (7 \times 3) \times 2$.

These equations illustrate a special case of the associative property for multiplication, which states that $a \times (b \times c) = (a \times b) \times c$. Specifically, in this case, $(2 \times 4) \times b = 2 \times (4 \times b)$ or $a \times (3 \times 2) = (a \times 3) \times 2$.

×	0	1	2	3	4	5	6	7	8	9
0	0	0	0	0	0	0	0	0	0	0
1	0	1	2	3	4	5	6	7	8	9
2	0	2	4	6	8	10	12	14	16	18
3	0	3	6	9	12	15	18	21	24	27
4	0	4	8	12	16	20	24	28	32	36
5	0	5	10	15	20	25	30	35	40	45
6	0	6	12	18	24	30	36	42	48	54
7	0	7	14	21	28	35	42	49	56	63
8	0	8	16	24	33	40	48	56	64	72
9	0	9	18	27	36	45	54	63	72	81

Students can notice, too, that multiplying a factor by n and dividing the other factor by that same amount n results in the same product. This is another way of stating the associative property, $(a \times b) \times c = a \times (b \times c)$, since to get from the left side of the equation to the right side, one divides the first factor, $a \times b$, by b to get a, and one multiplies the second factor, c, by b to get $b \times c$.

To see this principle in the table, a student might observe that the values in the 6 row (at least the multiples of 6 that are less than 20) appear in the 2 row as well, but are more spaced out in the 2 row. Highlighted on the next page, one sees that $6 \times 0 = 2 \times 0$ (since $(2 \times 3) \times 0 = 2 \times (3 \times 0)$), $6 \times 1 = 2 \times 3$ (since $(2 \times 3) \times 1 = 2 \times (3 \times 1)$), that $6 \times 2 = 2 \times 6$ (since $(2 \times 3) \times 2 = 2 \times (3 \times 2)$), and that $6 \times 3 = 2 \times 9$ (since $(2 \times 3) \times 3 = 2 \times (3 \times 3)$). Students could recognize that the products that are 1 space apart in the 6 row are 3 spaces apart in the 2 row (since the other factor was tripled).

×	0	1	2	3	4	5	6	7	8	9
0	0	0	0	0	0	0	0	0	0	0
1	0	1	2	3	4	5	6	7	8	9
2	0	2	4	6	8	10	12	14	16	18
3	0	3	6	9	12	15	18	21	24	27
4	0	4	8	12	16	20	24	28	32	36
5	0	5	10	15	20	25	30	35	40	45
6	0	6	12	18	24	30	36	42	48	54
7	0	7	14	21	28	35	42	49	56	63
8	0	8	16	24	33	40	48	56	64	72
9	0	9	18	27	36	45	54	63	72	81

Good Questions to Ask

- Ask students to examine the addition table to see how each of these ideas shows up in the table:

  - That adding 9 is the same as adding 8 and then 1,
  - That adding two odd numbers results in an even number,
  - That adding 8 to a number results in a sum that is 4 more than adding 4 to the original number, and
  - That there are lots of combinations of two counting numbers that add to 10, but fewer combinations of two counting numbers that add to 6.

  [*Answer:* For the first example, students might compare the numbers in the column under 9 to the numbers in the column under 8 and realize that they are 1 more each time. For the second example, students might notice that in any row starting with an odd number, every other number is even and those numbers are all in columns where the heading number is odd. For the third example, students might compare the values of the numbers in the column under 8 to those in the column under 4 and see that each number in the 8 column is 4 more than the number in the 4 column. For the fourth example, students might count how many 10s, versus 6s, appear in the body of the table.]

- Ask students to examine the multiplication table to see how each of these ideas shows up in the table. They should choose two of the patterns to explain.

  - That multiplying by 4 results in twice as much as multiplying by 2,
  - That multiplying an even number by an odd number results in an even number,

* That the products that result from multiplying numbers greater than 0 by 9 are numbers for which the sum of the digits is 9, and
* That 3 × a number less than 10 added to 4 × that same number less than 10 is always in the 7 row.

[*Answer:* For the first example, students might compare the numbers in the row labeled 4 to those in the row labeled 2 and see that the first number is always double the second. They can explain this because 4 groups of something is twice as much as 2 groups. For the second example, students might notice that all the numbers in a column with an even heading or a row with an even heading are even, even if the other heading is odd. For the third example, students might observe that the sum of the digits is 9 for all numbers in the 9 column or the 9 row. For the last example, students might add corresponding numbers in the 3 row and the 4 row and find the result in the 7 row. They might explain this using the distributive property.]

* Ask students why the numbers in the 6 row are 6 apart. [*Answer:* Students should realize that any number in the 6 row represents the total amount in 6 groups; if the group size is increased by 1 (which means going to the next column), there are 6 more 1s, which is a total of 6 more.]
* Ask students why the same numbers are in the 5 row as in the 5 column. [*Answer:* Students should realize, perhaps using an array model, that the order of numbers does not matter when one multiplies.]

Summary

By the end of Grade 3, students use equations to model adding and subtracting situations as well as multiplying and dividing situations or combinations involving several operations. These students are comfortable using letters to represent variables and solve equations in a variety of ways. They also recognize how patterns in arithmetic, particularly in the addition and multiplication tables, relate to the properties of the operations.

Arithmetic Generalizations

Number and Operations—Fractions	CCSSM 4.NF
Extend understanding of fraction equivalence and ordering.	

1. Explain why a fraction $\frac{a}{b}$ is equivalent to a fraction $\frac{n \times a}{n \times b}$ by using visual fraction models, with attention to how the number and size of the parts differ even though the two fractions themselves are the same size. Use this principle to recognize and generate equivalent fractions.

IMPORTANT UNDERLYING IDEAS

> **Generating equivalent fractions.** In earlier grades, students learned generalizations that allow them to rename numbers or expressions with other numbers or expressions. For example, they learned that $a \times b$ can be renamed as $b \times a$ and that $a + b$ can be renamed as $(a + c) + (b - c)$ regardless of the values of a, b, and c. These sorts of generalizations are an important component of algebraic thinking.

At this level, they learn another generalization—that any fraction $\frac{a}{b}$ can be renamed as $\frac{n \times a}{n \times b}$ for any values of a, b, and n other than a 0 value for n. This equivalence is, of course, useful when comparing fractions, adding them, subtracting them, or even multiplying or dividing them.

This concept can be explained to students using visuals that show how any equal subdivisions of the parts of a fraction leads to another name for that fraction. For example, $\frac{3}{5}$ becomes $\frac{6}{10}$ or $\frac{9}{15}$ in the diagram below by multiplying both numerator and denominator by either 2 or 3.

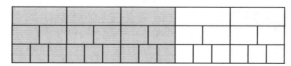

Notice that looking in reverse shows that the numerator and denominator can also be divided by the same amount to get an equivalent fraction, for example, dividing both numerator and denominator of $\frac{6}{10}$ by 2 to get $\frac{3}{5}$.

Good Questions to Ask

- We know that it is true that $\frac{a}{b} = \frac{n \times a}{n \times b}$. Is it also true that $\frac{a}{b} = \frac{a+n}{b+n}$? [**Answer:** No. For example, $\frac{2}{3}$ is not equal to $\frac{3}{4}$ (adding 1 to both numerator and denominator). But sometimes it is true, since $\frac{2}{2} = \frac{3}{3}$.]

- Why is every fraction with a numerator and a denominator that are even equivalent to a fraction where that is not true? [**Answer:** If the numerator and denominator are both even, one could keep dividing by 2 as many times as necessary until one of them becomes odd. For example, for $\frac{4}{8}$, one would divide by 2 to get $\frac{2}{4}$ and then again to get $\frac{1}{2}$. For $\frac{16}{30}$, one would divide by 2 to get $\frac{8}{15}$.]

Representing Situations Using Equations

Operations and Algebraic Thinking	CCSSM 4.OA

Use the four operations with whole numbers to solve problems.

1. Interpret a multiplication equation as a comparison, e.g., interpret $35 = 5 \times 7$ as a statement that 35 is 5 times as many as 7 and 7 times as many as 5. Represent verbal statements of multiplicative comparisons as multiplication equations.

2. Multiply or divide to solve word problems involving multiplicative comparison, e.g., by using drawings and equations with a symbol for the unknown number to represent the problem, distinguishing multiplicative comparison from additive comparison.

3. Solve multistep word problems posed with whole numbers and having whole-number answers using the four operations, including problems in which remainders must be interpreted. Represent these problems using equations with a letter standing for the unknown quantity. Assess the reasonableness of answers using mental computation and estimation strategies including rounding.

Number and Operations—Fractions	CCSSM 4.NF

Build fractions from unit fractions by applying and extending previous understandings of operations on whole numbers.

3. d. Solve word problems involving addition and subtraction of fractions referring to the same whole and having like denominators, e.g., by using visual fraction models and equations to represent the problem.

4. c. Solve word problems involving multiplication of a fraction by a whole number, e.g., by using visual fraction models and equations to represent the problem. For example, if each person at a party will eat $\frac{3}{8}$ of a pound of roast beef, and there will be 5 people at the party, how many pounds of roast beef will be needed? Between what two whole numbers does your answer lie?

IMPORTANT UNDERLYING IDEAS

> *Interpreting multiplication as comparison.* Although students are introduced to multiplication equations as a way of describing equal groups, they must broaden their understanding to other nuances of the concept of equal groups. For example, if one says that Paul has four times as many stickers as Alicia, the expression $4 \times a$ describes how many stickers Paul has. The equation $4 \times a = 20$ suggests that Paul has 20 stickers, and we want to know how many stickers Alicia has. The equation $4 \times 5 = p$ suggests that Alicia has 5 stickers and we want to know how many stickers Paul has.

The reason this multiplicative comparison is a "nuance" of equal groups is that we can think of Paul's amount as 4 equal groups of Alicia's amount even though, technically, there are no groups.

> *Choosing an appropriate equation.* When a student attempts to use an equation to describe a problem involving one of the four operations, she or he reveals an understanding of what the operations of addition, subtraction, multiplication, and division mean. Flexibility in interpretation of operations is important. Although subtraction can represent a take-away situation, it might also describe a comparison situation or a how-many-more-are-needed situation. Multiplication is often about a situation involving equal groups, but considering a multiplicative comparison is a slightly different interpretation. Division can be about sharing, but it can also be used in a multiplicative comparison. These operation meanings are consistent, whether the numbers involved are fractions or whole numbers.

Once a problem is modeled with an equation, students generally solve the equation to solve the problem. The process of solving the equation should involve using a model that reflects both the situation and the equation.

For example, for the equation $\frac{2}{3} + \Box = \frac{4}{3}$, the student might be thinking about how much more flour is needed than sugar if $\frac{2}{3}$ cup of flour and $1\frac{1}{3}$ cups of sugar are needed. The student is likely to model $\frac{2}{3}$ and add to it until $\frac{4}{3}$ is achieved. Alternately, the student might be thinking about how much flour is left if there was $1\frac{1}{3}$ cups initially and $\frac{2}{3}$ cup was used. This time, the student might choose to start with $1\frac{1}{3}$ cups and remove $\frac{2}{3}$ cup, but not necessarily.

For the equation $50 = 2 \times s$, the student should be realizing that 50 counters might be formed into 2 equal groups. However, for the equation $60 = g \times 4$, it makes sense to model lots of 4s being put together to make 60; the number of groups of 4 is counted.

For the equation $c \times \frac{3}{5} = \frac{18}{5}$, the student might be modeling enough jumps of $\frac{3}{5}$ on a number line to get from 0 to $\frac{18}{5}$. But for the equation $\frac{3}{5} \times c = \frac{18}{5}$, the student could be thinking about the size of a number that would allow $\frac{3}{5}$ of it to be a little more than $3\frac{1}{2}$.

If the equation comes from a word problem, the story can help the student make sense of what the equation means; if there is no story problem, the student essentially has to invent meaning when he or she sees an equation. For example, $40 - s = 10$ could mean that there were 40, some were taken away, 10 were left, and one wants to know how many were removed. But it could be asking how far to go back on a number line from 40 to get to 10. Or it could be asking how old someone is if someone who is 10 years older is 40.

➤ **Interpreting remainders.** Some students are comfortable solving equations such as $21 \div 3 = a$, but would argue that $22 \div 3 = a$ is not solvable. Such students simply do not understand how to handle a remainder in solving an equation. They are not aware of the conventions for expressing remainders.

Students need to gain experience in dealing with such equations. They might solve the equation as "about 7" or as $7\frac{1}{3}$ or perhaps as "7 Remainder 1."

➤ **Position of the unknown in an equation.** Students should have experiences solving multiplication equations of the form $a \times b = c$, where each of the variables a, b, or c is the unknown. For example, they might solve $a \times 4 = 20$, $4 \times b = 20$, or $4 \times 5 = c$.

The interpretation of these three equations is somewhat different. In the first instance, $a \times 4 = 20$, the student knows there are 20 items in groups of 4 and wants to know how many groups, or knows that one person has 4 items and one has 20 items and is looking for the "scale factor," that is, how many times as many as 4 the number 20 is. A model to show this could involve creating groups of 4 counters until 20 counters have been used and then counting the number of groups. Essentially this is a division question that asks how many of one unit in another.

In the second instance, $4 \times b = 20$, the student knows that there are 4 groups with a total of 20 items and wants to know how many are in a group, or knows that someone who has 20 items has 4 times as many as someone else and wants to know how many that other person has. This model involves building 4 groups and distributing items equally among the groups to determine how many items are in each group. Essentially, this is a division question involving sharing.

In the third instance, $4 \times 5 = c$, the student knows that there are 4 groups with 5 items in a group and wonders how many items there are in total, or knows that someone has 4 times as many items as someone with 5 items. This model involves building the groups and keeping count.

➤ **Importance of estimating solutions.** Just as it is valuable for students to estimate when performing a calculation to check the reasonableness of a calculated answer, it makes sense to encourage estimation of a solution to an equation as an important step in solving the equation.

For example, imagine that a student is solving this equation: $4 \times q + 3 = 31$. It would make sense for that student to first think: "q must be less than 10 since 4×10 is already 40 and that's too much. q must be more than 5 since 4×5 is 20, and 3 more is not 31. Then the actual answer of 7 seems reasonable."

If the equation were $3 \times p + 18 = 2 \times p + 47$, a student might realize that adding 47 to $2p$ gets one about 17 past $3p$, so the extra p must be worth about 30 ($47 - 17$).

If the equation were $\frac{3}{5} + j = 1$, the student might recognize that if a fraction greater than $\frac{1}{2}$ is added to another fraction and the result is 1, the other fraction must be less than $\frac{1}{2}$.

Estimation can be used either in place of, or in addition to, substituting the resulting solution in the equation to see if the equation is true. Substitution alone is not as good as also doing an estimation, since the student could make the same calculation error during the process of substituting and checking as was made during the process of solving. Such an error is less likely to go undetected if estimation is also used.

Good Questions to Ask

* Ask students to write an equation or an expression that would describe each situation:

  * Connor has three times as many cards as Liam.
  * Jenni has 80 stamps. That's 5 times as many as Sara. How many does Sara have?
  * Aisha has 5 times as many books as Laura. If Laura has 8, how many does Aisha have?
  * The perimeter of a certain square is 8 times as much as the perimeter of another square.
  * Some juice is added to $\frac{2}{3}$ cup to end up with 2 cups. How much was added?
  * You combine lots of $\frac{3}{4}$ cup of flour.

  [**Answer (examples):** The first statement might be written as the expression $3 \times l$ or as the equation $c = 3 \times l$. The second one might be written as $80 = 5 \times s$ or as $s = 80 \div 5$ or as $5 = 80 \div s$. The third one might be written as $5 \times 8 = a$ or as $8 \times 5 = a$ or as $a = 8 + 8 + 8 + 8 + 8$ or .... The fourth one might be written as the expression $8 \times p$ or as $n = 8 \times p$. The fifth one might be written as $\frac{2}{3} + j = 2$. The last one might be written as $j \times \frac{3}{4}$. Notice that equations are used, rather than expressions, when specific amounts are indicated as the results.]

* Ask a student to explain why 4×8 could mean the total count of 4 groups of 8 but could also mean 4 times as much as 8. [**Answer:** If you show 4 groups of 8, you are automatically showing 8 four times, and that is what "4 times as much as 8" means.]

- Ask students to model each equation:

$$4 \times s = 20$$
$$t \times 7 = 42$$
$$8 = 32 \div m$$
$$p = 50 \div 10$$

[**Answer:** For $4 \times s = 20$, the student might put out 20 items and try to form 4 groups. For $t \times 7 = 42$, the student might make groups of 7 out of 42 items and count the number of groups. For $8 = 32 \div m$, the student might put out 32 items and try to form 8 groups, counting the size of each group. For $p = 50 \div 10$, the student might draw a number line and hop back from 50 to 0, in hops of 10, counting the number of hops.]

- Ask students how the solutions for $24 \div 3 = n$ and $26 \div 3 = n$ are alike and different. [**Answer:** There are about 8 in a group each time, but in the first case all of the items are used up in making equal groups, and in the second case there are 2 items left over when the group sizes are equal.]

- Tell students that a problem is represented by the equation $4 \times t = 64$. Ask what the problem might have been. [**Answer:** One possibility is this: Jane had $64. That is 4 times as much as she used to have. How much did she have before?]

- Ask students to provide a good estimate for the solution of each equation. Instruct them *not* to solve the equation first. Also ask them to explain the reason for their estimate.

$$3 \times j - 4 = 26$$
$$52 + k = 94$$
$$103 - k = 22$$
$$96 \div s = 6$$
$$50 + 2 \times k = 32 + 4 \times k$$
$$\tfrac{3}{5} + s = \tfrac{12}{5}$$
$$6 \times \tfrac{a}{b} = 4$$

[**Answer:** The solution to $3 \times j - 4 = 26$ might be around 9, since 3×9 is close to 26 and 4 less is not that much less. The solution to $52 + k = 94$ might be about 40 since $52 + 40$ is close to 94. The solution to $103 - k = 22$ might be about 80 since if you take 80 from 100 you get 20. The solution to $96 \div s = 6$ might be about 15 since 96 is about halfway between 60 and 120, which are 6×10 and 6×20, and 15 is halfway between 10 and 20). The solution to $50 + 2 \times k = 32 + 4 \times k$ might be about 10 since having 2 more ks meant having a number about 20 less. The solution to $\tfrac{3}{5} + s = \tfrac{12}{5}$ might be about 2 since $\tfrac{12}{5}$ is more than 2 and $\tfrac{3}{5}$ is a little more than $\tfrac{1}{2}$. The solution to $6 \times \tfrac{a}{b} = 4$ might be a fraction a little more than $\tfrac{1}{2}$, such as $\tfrac{2}{3}$, since $6 \times \tfrac{1}{2}$ would not be enough and 6×1 would be too much.]

- Ask students for a multiplication equation where the solution is close to 5, but not exactly 5. [**Answer:** Some possibilities are $5 \times j = 26$; $4 \times k = 24$; $100 \times l = 510$.]

Pattern Rules

Operations and Algebraic Thinking	CCSSM 4.OA
Generate and analyze patterns.	

5. Generate a number or shape pattern that follows a given rule. Identify apparent features of the pattern that were not explicit in the rule itself. For example, given the rule "Add 3" and the starting number 1, generate terms in the resulting sequence and observe that the terms appear to alternate between odd and even numbers. Explain informally why the numbers will continue to alternate in this way.

IMPORTANT UNDERLYING IDEAS

➤ *Describing rules in alternate ways.* What makes a pattern a pattern is its regularity, or predictability. It is the rule that describes a mathematical pattern that makes its regularity apparent.

For example, the pattern 5, 8, 11, 14, 17, . . . can be described by the rule "Start with 5 and keep adding 3." The regularity is in the repeated addition of 3. An alternate description of this same pattern, which usually would be offered in a later grade, is that any term in the pattern can be determined by multiplying its position in the pattern by 3 and adding 2; for example, the 6th term is $3 \times 6 + 2 = 20$. Again, the predictability comes from the rule; knowing the rule allows you to predict any term in the pattern.

Just as the pattern 5, 8, 11, 14, 17, . . . above was described with two different rules, any pattern can be described in more than one way. For example, the pattern 2, 4, 6, 8, 10, . . . can be described with these pattern rules: "Start at 2 and keep adding 2" or "Multiply the position number by 2 to determine the term value" or "Start at 2, and each time add 3 and then subtract 1."

➤ *Deducing from pattern rules.* How a pattern rule is described always explicitly or implicitly tells us how that pattern grows. For example, the rule "Start at 5 and keep adding 2" explicitly tells us that the pattern grows by a value of 2 each time. The rule "Multiply the term position by 2 and then add 3" implicitly tells us that the pattern grows by a value of 2 each time. This is because $2 \times (n + 1) + 3$ is 2 more than $2 \times n + 3$.

Knowing how a pattern grows can tell us a number of things about it, for example:

- Which terms are odd or even,
- Whether the terms, or which terms, are multiples of 3, and
- When the pattern reaches a particular value, for example, 100.

For example, consider the pattern "Start at 6 and add 4 each time." Since you start at an even number and keep adding even numbers, all the terms have to be even. That is because any even number is made up of groups of 2, so starting with groups of 2 and adding more groups of 2 ensures that the result will be groups of 2.

Since you start at 6, and 6 is a multiple of 3, you know that there are some multiples of 3 in the pattern. But the pattern goes 6, 10, 14, 18, . . . , so once you are at a multiple of 3, you will not reach another multiple of 3 for another 3 terms. Notice that this finding continues: **6**, 10, 14, **18**, 22, 26, **30**, 34, 38, **42**, ... This makes sense; adding 4 three times is like adding 12. Since 12 is a multiple of 3, it is made up of groups of 3. If you keep adding groups of 3 to a number that is already made up of 3s, you have another multiple of 3. A student could conclude that the first number and every subsequent third number is a multiple of 3.

Since you start at 6, and keep adding 4 each time, you will not get to 100 until the 25th term. That is because if you add 23 fours to 6 (to get to the 24th term), you are up to $6 + 23 \times 4 = 98$, so you need one more term to get to 100.

Other patterns involving whole numbers can be analyzed in similar ways to look for multiples of other numbers (not necessarily 2 or 3), as well. For example, you know that the pattern 7, 13, 19, 25, 31, . . . contains no multiples of 6 since it begins at 1 more than a multiple of 6 and you keep adding 6s; there will always be a remainder of 1 when you divide by 6.

> **Comparing patterns.** One of the aspects of patterns mathematicians are particularly interested in studying is how fast they grow. Patterns are often compared in terms of how fast they grow rather than where they begin. For example, eventually students need to realize that no matter where a pattern starts, a pattern that grows by 3 ultimately surpasses a pattern that grows by 2, or that a pattern that grows by multiplying by a positive whole number greater than 1 ultimately surpasses a pattern that grows by adding a positive whole number.

These examples of pattern growth could be explored by having students compare, for example, the pattern 4, 7, 10, 13, 16, . . . to the pattern 100, 102, 104, 106, . . . or the pattern 1, 2, 4, 8, 16, 32, . . . to the pattern 200, 206, 212, 218, 224, ...

In the first case, 4, 7, 10, 13, . . . starts behind 100, 102, ... but by the 100th term, the first pattern gets to $4 + 99 \times 3 = 301$ and the second gets to only $100 + 99 \times 2 = 298$. Since the first pattern grows faster, it will stay ahead after the 100th term.

In the second case, 1, 2, 4, 8, 16, 32, . . . surpasses 200, 206, 212, 218, 224, . . . by the 10th term. The 10th term in the first pattern has already reached 512, whereas the second pattern's 10th term is only 254.

This sort of pattern exploration provides a good opportunity for students to practice computational skills as well as to make mathematical generalizations.

Good Questions to Ask

* Ask students to describe at least one or two alternative rules for each pattern:

  * Pattern 1: Start at 6 and keep adding 6.
  * Pattern 2: Start at 4 and keep adding 9.
  * Pattern 3: Start at 10 and keep adding 5.

  [*Answer (examples)*: *Pattern 1*: Start at 6, add 3 and then 3 more to get the next term each time. Multiply the position of the number in the pattern by 6.

  Pattern 2: Start at 4 and add 10 and then subtract 1 to get the next number each time. Multiply the position of the number in the pattern by 9 and then subtract 5.

  Pattern 3: Add 1 to the position of the number in the pattern and then multiply by 5. Multiply the position of the number in the pattern by 5 and then add 5.]

* Provide several pattern rules to students. Ask them to tell as much as they can about what they notice about the numbers in the pattern. Suggest that they consider both size (how big the numbers are) and properties of the numbers such as whether they are even or odd, multiples of 10 or not, etc. They should explain why what they notice happens.

  * Pattern 1: Start at 8 and keep adding 5.
  * Pattern 2: Start at 4 and keep adding 7.
  * Pattern 3: Start at 100 and keep subtracting 3.
  * Pattern 4: Start at 4 and keep doubling.

  [*Answer (examples)*: *Pattern 1*: Numbers alternate between even and odd since they start even. By adding 5, the next term switches to odd, but adding 5 again is like adding 10, so the result is back to even. There are no multiples of 5 or 10 since the starting number is a non-multiple and the added groups are 5s. It takes 20 terms to get up to 100 since 19 × 5 = 95 and 95 + 8 is more than 100. That means that 5 has to be added 19 times, getting to the 20th term.]

* Ask students to compare the pattern 5, 8, 11, 14, 17, 20, . . . (Start at 5 and keep adding 3) to each of the patterns below. They should talk about how the patterns are alike and how they differ, considering how fast they grow, what kinds of numbers the patterns include, and how knowing about one pattern helps one to know about the other. This will be an example of the mathematical practice standard of reasoning abstractly and quantitatively.

  * Pattern 1: 7, 10, 13, 16, 19, . . . (Start at 7 and keep adding 3)
  * Pattern 2: 5, 7, 9, 11, 13, 15, . . . (Start at 5 and keep adding 2)
  * Pattern 3: 5, 15, 45, 135, . . . (Start at 5 and keep multiplying by 3)

  [*Answer (examples)*: *Pattern 1*: The 7, 10, 13, . . . pattern is always 2 ahead of the 5, 8, 11, . . . pattern. Both patterns alternate between odd numbers and even numbers in the same way. The pattern starting at 7 gets to 10 and 100 one term before the pattern that starts at 5. Both patterns have no multiples of 3. Both patterns have multiples of 4 that are 4 apart.

   Pattern 2: The 5, 8, 11, . . . pattern starts at the same place as the 5, 7, 9, . . . pattern but grows faster. The 5, 8, 11, . . . pattern alternates between even and odd numbers, but the 5, 7, 9, . . . pattern is all odd numbers. The 5, 8, 11, . . . pattern has no multiples of 3 in it, but the 5, 7, 9, . . . pattern does (e.g., 9 and 15).

   Pattern 3: The 5, 15, 45, 135, . . . pattern starts at the same place as the 5, 8, 11, 14, . . . pattern, but the multiplying pattern gets bigger much faster. The multiplying pattern has only odd numbers in it, but the adding pattern has odds and evens.]

Solving Measurement Problems with Equations

Measurement and Data	CCSSM 4.MD
Solve problems involving measurement and conversion of measurements from a larger unit to a smaller unit.	

1. Know relative sizes of measurement units within one system of units including km, m, cm; kg, g; lb, oz; l, ml; hr, min, sec. Within a single system of measurement, express measurements in a larger unit in terms of a smaller unit. Record measurement equivalents in a two-column table. For example, know that 1 ft is 12 times as long as 1 in. Express the length of a 4 ft snake as 48 in. Generate a conversion table for feet and inches listing the number pairs (1, 12), (2, 24), (3, 36), ...

2. Use the four operations to solve word problems involving distances, intervals of time, liquid volumes, masses of objects, and money, including problems involving simple fractions or decimals, and problems that require expressing measurements given in a larger unit in terms of a smaller unit. Represent measurement quantities using diagrams such as number line diagrams that feature a measurement scale.

3. Apply the area and perimeter formulas for rectangles in real world and mathematical problems. For example, find the width of a rectangular room given the area of the flooring and the length, by viewing the area formula as a multiplication equation with an unknown factor.

IMPORTANT UNDERLYING IDEAS

> ➤ *Converting from one unit to another.* The relationship between two measurement units can be thought of in terms of solving an equation with a missing term. For example, since 1 foot = 12 inches, if one knows that the number of inches is 150

and wants the number of feet, one would be solving the equation $f = 150 \div 12$ or the equation $12 \times f = 150$.

Although expressing such a conversion as an equation might seem to be over-complicating a simple calculation, it will be helpful as the student goes up the grades to know how to algebraically model a wide variety of situations, including these measurement situations.

> *Modeling measurement problems.* Many word problems involve measurement situations. As with other story problems, students can often solve the problems by first modeling them with an equation and then solving the equation. A few examples of modeling problems with equations are shown below:

  * The perimeter of a square is 84 inches. What is the side length? (*Example:* $84 = 4 \times s$)
  * Jane's mother drove 52 miles to her job and the same distance home. How far did she drive in total? (*Example:* $d = 52 + 52$)
  * Three identical boxes were placed on a scale, and the total weight was 78 pounds. How much did each box weigh? (*Example:* $3 \times b = 78$)

> *Formulas for area and perimeter of rectangles.* Essentially, measurement formulas are equations that relate different variables, which happen to be measures. We often substitute known values of certain variables to get unknown values of another variable.

For example, the formula $P = 2 \times l + 2 \times w$ is an equation that relates the perimeter to the length and width of a rectangle. It is a statement that is true for any values of P, l, and w. If one knows two of the values, the equation can be used to help determine the third. For example, if one knows that a rectangle has width 4" and perimeter 20", one can determine length by solving the equation $20 = 2 \times l + 2 \times 4$, or $20 = 2 \times l + 8$.

Applying measurement formulas is a very useful way to practice algebraic skills. Using formulas helps students not only to calculate measurements but also to see when equations are used, to practice how they are solved, and to recognize the difference between equations that state a relationship between variables and those with a focus on solving for a missing value.

Good Questions to Ask

* Ask students to describe what table of values they might create to convert cubic yards to cubic feet. Then ask if they think the table would be more useful or less useful than an equation relating cubic yards to cubic feet. [*Answer (example):* I would make a table with 1 matching 27, 2 matching 54, 3 matching 81, etc.

I think the equation is easier since it works even if the numbers are not whole numbers, such as $2\frac{1}{2}$ or $3\frac{1}{4}$.]

- Ask students to describe an equation they might use to convert kilometers to meters. Ask why the equation is correct. [**Answer (example):** meters = 1,000 × kilometers. I used this equation because 1 km = 1,000 m, so you multiply the number of kilometers you have by 1,000 to get the number of meters.]

- Ask students for two different equations to model this measurement problem: Kyle walked $1\frac{1}{2}$ miles on Monday and double that on Tuesday. How far did he walk altogether? [**Answer:** One of the equations could be $1\frac{1}{2} + 2 \times 1\frac{1}{2} = d$.]

- Tell students you used the equation $d = 250 \div 5$ to model a problem about distance. Ask what the problem might have been. [**Answer (example):** We drove 250 miles in 5 hours. How far did we drive each hour?]

- Ask students to create a measurement problem involving capacity in quarts. Then ask them to create and solve an equation that would model the problem. [**Answer (example):** A pot held $4\frac{1}{4}$ quarts of water. How many cups of water is that? Equation: $4\frac{1}{4} \times 4 = c$. The answer is 17 cups.]

- Ask students for an equation they could solve to determine the length of a room with a width of 12 feet and an area of 180 square feet. [**Answer (example):** 180 = 12 × *l*.]

- Ask students to explain why the formula for the area of a rectangle involves two variables (length and width) but the formula for the area of a square involves only one variable (side length). [**Answer:** For a rectangle that is not a square, the length and width are different, so the area formula has to consider both of those amounts. But since a square has a length that is the same as its width, once one is known the other is automatically known, so both are not needed in the formula.]

Summary

By the end of Grade 4, students use equations to represent more complex problems and a wider variety of problems than in earlier grades. These problems could involve fractions or whole numbers and they could involve combinations of operations. Students are comfortable solving equations involving multiple meanings of multiplication and division of whole numbers, as well as equations involving addition and subtraction of fractions where the missing unknown is located in different spots in the equation.

Grade 4 students might use equations to help them convert measurements or describe measurement formulas. They also see the relationship between the specifics of the pattern rule for a particular pattern and the types of numbers that appear in that pattern as well as the pattern's growth.

GRADE 5

Analyzing Patterns

Operations and Algebraic Thinking	CCSSM 5.OA
Analyze patterns and relationships.	

3. Generate two numerical patterns using two given rules. Identify apparent relationships between corresponding terms. Form ordered pairs consisting of corresponding terms from the two patterns, and graph the ordered pairs on a coordinate plane. For example, given the rule "Add 3" and the starting number 0, and given the rule "Add 6" and the starting number 0, generate terms in the resulting sequences, and observe that the terms in one sequence are twice the corresponding terms in the other sequence. Explain informally why this is so.

IMPORTANT UNDERLYING IDEAS

> *Comparing patterns numerically.* Linear patterns are ones that increase by the same amount each term. These patterns are particularly useful in describing many real-world situations. They differ only in where they start and how fast they grow.

Eventually students should realize that no matter where a pattern starts, a pattern that grows more quickly ultimately surpasses a pattern that grows more slowly. This could be explored by having students compare, for example, the pattern 1, 6, 11, 16, 21, 26, ..., which grows by 5 but starts at 1, with the pattern 100, 102, 104, 106, ..., which grows by only 2 but starts all the way at 100. Eventually, the first pattern surpasses the second. In this case, the 35th number in the first pattern is 171 and the 35th number in the second pattern is 168. Once that point is reached, the numbers in the first pattern remain greater since they increase faster.

Notice that it might be difficult, in this case, for students to use the values in one pattern to predict the matching values in the second pattern. (There is in fact a way, but it is fairly complicated—add 4 to the number in Pattern 1, take $\frac{2}{5}$ of it, and then add 98. For example, the third number in Pattern 1 is 11, so the third number in the second pattern would be $\frac{2}{5}$ of $(4 + 11) + 98 = 104$.)

However, if both patterns start at 0, predicting the terms of one linear pattern by knowing the matching term in another is much easier. For example, when comparing 3, 6, 9, 12, 15, . . . to 5, 10, 15, 20, . . . , a student might realize that dividing by 3 and then multiplying by 5 matches any number in Pattern 1 to its counterpart in Pattern 2. This is because the rule for Pattern 1 is $3 \times n$, where n is the term position, and the rule for Pattern 2 is $5 \times n$, where n is the term position. Notice that dividing $3 \times n$ by 3 results in n and multiplying that result by 5 leads to $5 \times n$.

➤ **Comparing patterns graphically.** Often a visual representation of a mathematical relationship is more compelling for students than a tabular or numeric representation. If, for example, one wants students to understand that one pattern grows more quickly than another or to understand the relationship between two patterns, a graphical representation can be helpful.

For example, the graph below makes it quite visible that the values in the numerical pattern 4, 8, 12, 16, 20, . . . , which grows by 4s and is shown using black dots, are exactly $\frac{2}{3}$ of the values in the numerical pattern 6, 12, 18, 24, . . . , which grows by 6s and is shown using gray dots. Notice that in each vertical column, the black dot is $\frac{2}{3}$ of the way from the horizontal axis to the gray dot.

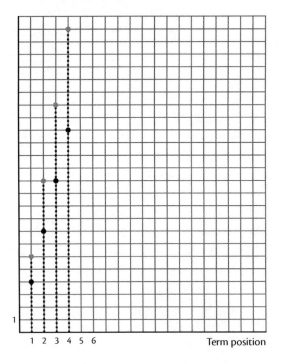

Although the graph on the next page does not make it as clear how the two matching pattern values are related, it does clarify when the pattern 1, 4, 7, 10, . . . , which grows by 3s, will overtake the pattern 23, 25, 27, 29, . . . , which grows by 2s.

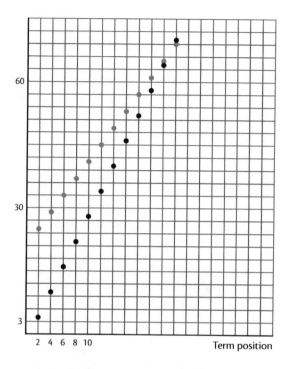

Term position

Good Questions to Ask

* Ask students to create two patterns, one of which whose terms are exactly three times the matching terms in the other one. Then ask them to make observations about how the patterns are alike and different. [**Answer (example):** The patterns might be 3, 6, 9, 12, 15, . . . and 9, 18, 27, 36, ... Both patterns alternate odd and even values. Both patterns grow by a constant amount. Both patterns are multiplication tables. Every number in the second pattern is in the first one, but later in the pattern.]

* Ask students to create two patterns such that the values in the second pattern can easily be predicted by knowing the values in the first one and to tell how the prediction is made. Then have them graph both patterns, and ask them how the graphs are useful in making the prediction. Point out how this is an example of the mathematical practice standard of reasoning abstractly and quantitatively. [**Answer (example):** 4, 7, 10, 13, 16, . . . and 14, 17, 20, 23, 26, ... One only needs to add 10 to the number in the first pattern to get the number in the second pattern. On the graphs, the second pattern's values are consistently 10 above the first pattern's values.]

* Ask students to tell as much as they can about the pattern 4, 9, 14, 19, 24, 29, ... Then ask them to create another pattern by adding 1 to each value and taking $\frac{3}{5}$ of the new amount. Ask what they notice about this new pattern. Finally, have them graph both patterns, and ask how the graphs show the relationship between the two and why this makes sense. [**Answer (example):** The first pattern's values

increase by 5 each time; the terms alternate between even and odd. The ones digit is always 4 or 9. The second pattern is 3, 6, 9, 12, 15, 18, ... The values increase by 3 each time. The terms alternate between odd and even. The ones digit could be anything. The same tens digits appears in at least three terms. On the graphs, the first pattern is above the second one each time, and the difference keeps getting larger. This makes sense because if the second number is close to $\frac{3}{5}$ of the first one, instead of going up by 5s, it should go up by $\frac{3}{5}$ of 5, which is 3. Since the second pattern goes up more slowly, the first pattern will keep getting more and more ahead of the second one.]

Using Equations to Represent and Solve Problems

Number and Operations—Fractions	CCSSM 5.NF
Use equivalent fractions as a strategy to add and subtract fractions.	
2. Solve word problems involving addition and subtraction of fractions referring to the same whole, including cases of unlike denominators, e.g., by using visual fraction models or equations to represent the problem. Use benchmark fractions and number sense of fractions to estimate mentally and assess the reasonableness of answers. For example, recognize an incorrect result $\frac{2}{5} + \frac{1}{2} = \frac{3}{7}$, by observing that $\frac{3}{7} < \frac{1}{2}$.	
Apply and extend previous understandings of multiplication and division to multiply and divide fractions.	
6. Solve real world problems involving multiplication of fractions and mixed numbers, e.g., by using visual fraction models or equations to represent the problem.	
7. c. Solve real world problems involving division of unit fractions by non-zero whole numbers and division of whole numbers by unit fractions, e.g., by using visual fraction models and equations to represent the problem. For example, how much chocolate will each person get if 3 people share $\frac{1}{2}$ lb of chocolate equally? How many $\frac{1}{3}$-cup servings are in 2 cups of raisins?	

IMPORTANT UNDERLYING IDEAS

> *Representing a problem with an equation.* Although students learn the operations of addition, subtraction, multiplication, and division with fractions and mixed numbers, they often do not know when to apply those operations. That is probably the most important thing to learn—when does it make sense to subtract two fractions? to multiply two fractions? to divide a whole number by a fraction? to divide a fraction by a whole number?

As students write equations to solve problems, it is useful if the equation closely matches the situation described in the problem. For example, if a problem states that a gas tank is $\frac{1}{3}$ full and asks how much more is needed to make a trip that takes about $\frac{7}{8}$ tank of gas, the student might write $\frac{1}{3} + \square = \frac{7}{8}$.

If a problem inquires about the number of $\frac{1}{3}$ cupfuls of flour required to measure out 2 cups of flour, then the equation $2 \div \frac{1}{3} = \square$ would make sense. If a problem asks how 4 people might equally share a prize that is $\frac{1}{5}$ of the entire raffle winnings, the student could use the equation $\frac{1}{5} \div 4 = \square$. If a problem asks about the area of a closet that is $3\frac{1}{3}$ feet by $4\frac{1}{2}$ feet, the equation $3\frac{1}{3} \times 4\frac{1}{2} = \square$ would be appropriate.

A student might choose a situation involving multiplication as comparison. A problem might be, for example, determining the amount of liquid needed in a recipe that normally requires $3\frac{1}{2}$ cups of water if the amounts are all multiplied by $\frac{2}{3}$. The equation would be $\frac{2}{3} \times 3\frac{1}{2} = \square$.

> **Flexibility in representations.** It should be a goal that students realize that any word problem that can be represented by an equation can be represented by more than one possible equation. For example, a problem that asks how many ribbons 8" long could be cut from a piece of ribbon 4' long could be modeled in terms of feet as $4 \div \frac{2}{3} = \square$ or as $\square \times \frac{2}{3} = 4$; alternatively, using inches instead of feet, possible models are $48 \div 8 = \square$ or $8 \times \square = 48$.

One way to encourage this flexibility among students is to regularly ask them to provide alternate equations.

Good Questions to Ask

* Ask students to create real-life problems to match fraction equations. For example, ask students what situation would have led one to write each of these equations.

$$\frac{3}{4} + \frac{2}{3} = \square$$

$$\frac{3}{4} - \frac{2}{3} = \square$$

$$\frac{2}{3} + \square = \frac{3}{4}$$

$$\frac{2}{3} \times \frac{3}{4} = \square$$

$$3 \div \frac{1}{3} = \square$$

$$\frac{4}{5} \times \square = 16$$

$$\frac{1}{8} \div 3 = \square$$

[*Answer (examples):*
  * I used $\frac{3}{4}$ cup of flour and then added $\frac{2}{3}$ cup more flour. How much flour did I use?
  * I had two recipes. One used $\frac{3}{4}$ cup of sugar and one used $\frac{2}{3}$ cup. How much more sugar did the first recipe use?

◆ My gas tank was $\frac{2}{3}$ full. I didn't have much money, and I put in a bit of gas. Now the tank is $\frac{3}{4}$ full. What fraction of a tank of gas did I add?

◆ $\frac{3}{4}$ of the kids in the school decided to participate in some intramurals. $\frac{2}{3}$ of those kids were boys. What fraction of students in the whole school were boys playing intramurals?

◆ I was cooking a turkey for 3 hours and checked it every $\frac{1}{3}$ of an hour. How many times did I check it?

◆ Only $\frac{4}{5}$ of the houses on the street were brick. If there were 16 brick houses, how many houses were on the street?

◆ A big urn was $\frac{1}{8}$ full, but I only used $\frac{1}{3}$ of what was in it. What fraction of the whole urn's capacity did I use?]

• Provide various fractional equations of the forms $\frac{a}{b} + \frac{c}{d} = \Box$, $\frac{a}{b} - \frac{c}{d} = \Box$, $\frac{a}{b} \times \frac{c}{d} = \Box$, $\frac{1}{b} \div c = \Box$, and $c \div \frac{1}{b} = \Box$. Ask students to write several equivalent equations for each. [**Answer (examples):** $6 \div \frac{1}{2} = \Box$ could be rewritten as $\frac{1}{2} \times \Box = 6$. $\frac{5}{8} - \frac{1}{3} = \Box$ could be rewritten as $\frac{1}{3} + \Box = \frac{5}{8}$. $\frac{3}{5} + \frac{1}{4} = \Box$ could be rewritten as $\Box - \frac{1}{4} = \frac{3}{5}$.]

• Tell students that various problems were created to match the equation $10 \div \frac{1}{5} = \Box$. Ask what has to be the same about all of those problems, as well as what could be different. [**Answer (example):** All of the problems involved the number 10 and the number $\frac{1}{5}$ in some fashion. Somehow the 10 was the whole and there were groups of $\frac{1}{5}$. Either we were counting how many groups of $\frac{1}{5}$ we had or we knew the size of $\frac{1}{5}$ of a unit and wanted to know the size of the whole unit. For example, a problem could have been about how many batches of a recipe that required $\frac{1}{5}$ cup of something we could make if we had a total of 10 cups. Or a problem could involve knowing we could do 10 things in $\frac{1}{5}$ of an hour and wondering how many things we could do in a whole hour (assuming we did the same thing over and over).]

Solving Measurement Problems with Equations

Measurement and Data	CCSSM 5.MD
Geometric measurement: understand concepts of volume and relate volume to multiplication and to addition.	

5. Relate volume to the operations of multiplication and addition and solve real world and mathematical problems involving volume.

   b. Apply the formulas $V = l \times w \times h$ and $V = b \times h$ for rectangular prisms to find volumes of right rectangular prisms with whole-number edge lengths in the context of solving real world and mathematical problems.

IMPORTANT UNDERLYING IDEAS

> *Formulas for volumes of rectangular prisms.* Essentially, measurement formulas are equations that relate different variables. Known values of certain variables are often substituted to get unknown values of another variable.

For example, the formula $V = l \times w \times h$ is an equation that is true for any values of V, l, w, and h for a rectangular prism. However, if one knows three specific values, the equation can be used to help determine the fourth. For example, if a rectangular prism has a volume of 60 cubic inches, a width of 3 inches, and a height of 5 inches, one can deduce that $60 = l \times 15$, so the length must be 4 inches.

Students might solve multiplication or division questions involving volumes of rectangular prisms. They are likely to use multiplication when they know the three linear dimensions, or the area of the base and the height, and want to find the volume. They are likely to use division when they know the volume and some of the linear dimensions or the area of the base and want the other dimensions.

Using measurement formulas is a very useful way to practice algebraic skills. It helps students not only to calculate measurements but also to see when equations are used, practice how they are solved, and recognize the difference between equations that state a relationship between variables and those in which the focus is solving for a missing value.

Good Questions to Ask

* Ask students for an equation to model the following measurement problem: A rectangular prism has a volume of 30 in³. If the length and width are doubled, but the height remains the same, what is the volume of the new prism? [*Answer (example):* V (of the larger prism) $= 2 \times l \times 2 \times w \times h$. Since V (of the original prism) $= l \times w \times h = 30$, for the larger prism $V = 2 \times 2 \times 30$.]

* Tell students you used the equation $d = 250 \div 5$ to model a problem about the volume of a rectangular prism. Ask what the problem might have been. [*Answer (example):* A rectangular prism has a volume of 250 cubic units. If the height is 5 units, what is the area of the base?]

* Ask students to create a measurement problem involving the volume of a rectangular prism that does not simply give the specific values of the length, width, and height. Then ask them to create and solve an equation that would model the problem. [*Answer (example):* I built a rectangular prism whose height is double its width. If the length of the base is 10 inches and the volume is 180 cubic inches, what are the width and the height? Equation: $180 = 10 \times w \times 2 \times w$ or $180 = 20 \times w \times w$; the answer is 3 inches for the width and 6 inches for the height.]

* Ask students for an equation they might solve to determine the height of a rectangular prism that is very tall and has a volume of 100 cubic units. Ask them to explain the equation. [*Answer (example):* $100 = h \times 2$. I knew that the base

area had to be small for the height to be tall, so I used a length of 2 and width of 1 for the base.]

• Ask students to explain why the formula for the volume of a rectangular prism involves three variables (length, width, and height) but the formula for the volume of a cube could be stated using only one variable (side length). [**Answer (example):** For a prism that is not a cube, the length, width, and height could be different, so the volume formula has to consider all three of those amounts. But since the length of a cube has to be the same as its width and height, once one of the measurements is known, the others are automatically also known, so all three are not needed in the formula.]

Using a Coordinate Grid to Visualize Algebraic Relationships

Geometry	CCSSM 5.G

Graph points on the coordinate plane to solve real world and mathematical problems.

1. Use a pair of perpendicular number lines, called axes, to define a coordinate system, with the intersection of the lines (the origin) arranged to coincide with the 0 on each line and a given point in the plane located by using an ordered pair of numbers, called its coordinates. Understand that the first number indicates how far to travel from the origin in the direction of one axis, and the second number indicates how far to travel in the direction of the second axis, with the convention that the names of the two axes and the coordinates correspond (e.g., x-axis and x-coordinate, y-axis and y-coordinate).

2. Represent real world and mathematical problems by graphing points in the first quadrant of the coordinate plane, and interpret coordinate values of points in the context of the situation.

IMPORTANT UNDERLYING IDEAS

> *Direction of travel from the origin.* When students consider plotting the ordered pair (a, b), they need to realize that they have choices about how to move to that position from the origin. They could, for example:

• Start at (0,0), move a spaces to the right and then b spaces directly up from that position,

• Start at (0,0), move b spaces up and then a spaces directly to the right from that position,

- Start at $(a,0)$ and then move b spaces directly up, or
- Start at $(0,b)$ and then move a spaces directly to the right.

Although one might think it best to be consistent, eventually students will want the flexibility of moving in any of these four ways to locate a point.

Students can then starting moving from one point to another. For example, they might move from (5,1) to (7,3) by plotting both points and noticing that 7 is 2 spaces to the right and 3 is 2 spaces up. Or they might just plot (5,1) and immediately realize they could go 2 spaces to the right and 2 spaces up to reach (7,3).

It is equally important that the students recognize that the position of (a,b) is typically not the same as the position of (b,a). The only exception is when $a = b$.

> **Representing problems on a coordinate plane.** Problems that are suitable for graphing in the first quadrant of a coordinate plane involve situations in which the values of two variables are related and each value is positive. The purpose of the graph is to display that relationship, as well as to serve as a tool for solving problems involving the two variables in the relationship. At the 5th-grade level, simple linear relationships make the most sense to investigate.

Often tables of values are created to describe specific instances of a relationship, those values are used to plot some points, and then students use the graph to interpolate and extrapolate.

For example, to show the relationship between the number of days in a certain number of weeks, students might create a table that pairs different numbers of weeks with the corresponding numbers of days and then plot those points as ordered pairs, using the two values in each row of the table as the coordinates.

Weeks	Days
1	7
2	14
3	21
4	28
5	35
6	42
7	49

Students need to learn that they have choices about which variable to put in which column, but that the choice affects the look of the graph. They also need to learn that they have choices in how the values of the variable in any column increase, but that often it is easier to notice patterns if those values increase in consistent ways, for example, by 1 each time or by 2 each time.

For example, none of the tables of values below is incorrect, even though some reveal patterns in the relationship between days and weeks better than others.

Days	Weeks
7	1
14	2
21	3
28	4
35	5
42	6
49	7

Weeks	Days
1	7
3	21
5	35
7	49
9	63
11	77
13	91

Weeks	Days
1	7
2	14
4	28
5	35
10	70
12	84
20	140

Once the points are plotted, students will likely notice the "linear" pattern and then can apply that pattern to extend the graph and use it to determine specific values of one variable in terms of the other.

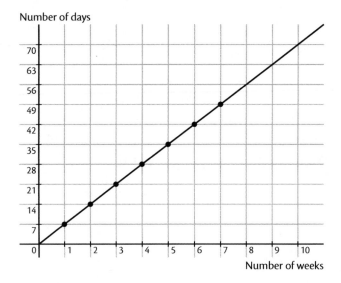

For example, as shown at the top of the next page, students could move directly up from (8,0) to look for the y-coordinate that is on the line by looking over to the left; that tells them how many days there are in 8 weeks.

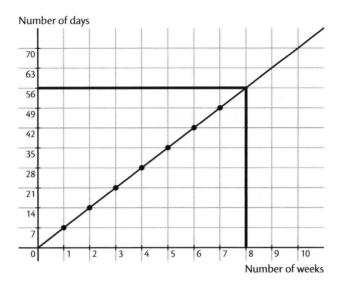

Students could also start at a *y*-value (number of days), move across to intersect the line, and determine the number of weeks for that number of days (see below). For example, by starting at (0,63) and going over and down, a student could determine that 63 days is 9 weeks.

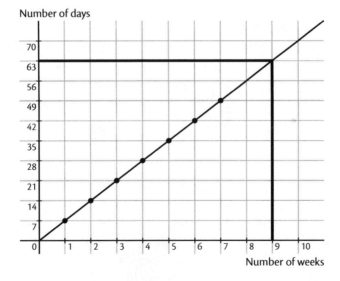

Many students are more comfortable using tables of values than graphs, but the graphical approach should be encouraged to get them accustomed to it. Later, graphs will be very valuable and useful to students.

Good Questions to Ask

* Ask students to describe how they would move:

    ✦ To the point (3,4) from (0,0),
    ✦ To the point (5,1) from (4,0), and
    ✦ To the point (6,3) from the point (8,4).

* Ask students to describe how the position of (5,2) is different from the position of (2,5). [***Answer (example):*** (5,2) is farther to the right and farther down than (2,5).]
* Ask students to consider the relationship between a number of people and the number of eyes that many people have. Encourage them to create a table of values and plot some of the points on a graph to model the relationship. Then ask them to create and solve a problem by using their graph. [***Answer (example):*** If students plot the points (1,2), (2,4), and (3,6) for the number of eyes for 1, 2, and 3 people, they might graph a line where the *y*-coordinate is twice the *x*-coordinate and determine that there are 20 people if there are 40 eyes.]
* Ask students to create a table of values relating the number of nickels to the number of cents they are worth. Then have them switch which variable is represented by the *x*-coordinate and which by the *y*-coordinate. Have them decide whether a problem asking about that relationship can be solved using either graph and explain why. [***Answer:*** Students should note that either graph can be used. For example, to decide how many cents correspond to 12 nickels, on one graph one can begin at (12,0), go up to the "line," and look across to find the number of cents. On the other graph, one can begin at (0,12), go to the right to the "line," and look down to find the number of cents.]

Summary

By the end of Grade 5, students use equations to represent situations involving addition, subtraction, and multiplication of fractions (even with different denominators), as well as limited situations involving fraction division. They use equations to describe measurement situations involving volumes of rectangular prisms. They show increasingly more flexibility in working with equations by representing problems in different ways and solving equations in different ways.

These students also use algebraic thinking to compare patterns both numerically and graphically by using properties of operations and to model relationships between variables by using coordinate grids.

GRADE 6

Observing Proportional Relationships

Ratios and Proportional Relationships	CCSSM 6.RP
Understand ratio concepts and use ratio reasoning to solve problems.	

2. Understand the concept of a unit rate $\frac{a}{b}$ associated with a ratio $a:b$ with $b \neq 0$, and use rate language in the context of a ratio relationship. For example, "This recipe has a ratio of 3 cups of flour to 4 cups of sugar, so there is $\frac{3}{4}$ cup of flour for each cup of sugar." "We paid \$75 for 15 hamburgers, which is a rate of \$5 per hamburger."

3. Use ratio and rate reasoning to solve real-world and mathematical problems, e.g., by reasoning about tables of equivalent ratios, tape diagrams, double number line diagrams, or equations.

   a. Make tables of equivalent ratios relating quantities with whole-number measurements, find missing values in the tables, and plot the pairs of values on the coordinate plane. Use tables to compare ratios.

IMPORTANT UNDERLYING IDEAS

> ***Using tables of values.*** Students are exposed to many linear relationships in their study of mathematics. For example, they might use the idea that each minute is 60 seconds, that each week is 7 days, that each foot is 12 inches, that each meter is 100 cm, that each mile is 5,280 feet, that each dollar is 4 quarters, etc.

Equivalent ratios or rates can be used to describe any one of these linear relationships in a variety of ways. For example, when comparing minutes to seconds, the rates 60:1, 120:2, and 180:3 all appropriately describe the relationship between seconds and minutes, although the unit rate 60:1 is often favored. Equivalent ratios or rates are often generated by using tables of values. For example, the relationship between dollars and the equivalent number of quarters might be represented as shown at the top of the next page. The equivalent ratios are 1:4, 2:8, 3:12, etc., or 4:1, 8:2, 12:3, etc.

Dollars	Quarters
0	0
1	4
2	8
3	12
4	16
5	20

Students might use the ratios in a table of values as sets of ordered pairs to graph on a coordinate grid. When these sorts of relationships are used, the graphs always form lines that go through the origin. In this particular case, a continuous line would not make sense since there can only be whole numbers of quarters.

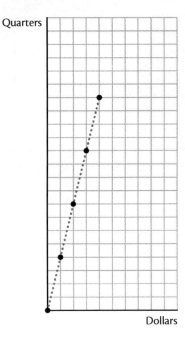

If, however, the relationship between minutes and hours were shown, it would make sense to use a continuous line; fractions of minutes and hours are meaningful.

In 6th grade, it is appropriate to provide students with some values for the equivalent ratios or rates in a table of values, but not all of them. Students could be asked to determine missing values. For example, in the table at the top of the next page, students might be asked to determine the values for the ?s if the values in the table describe equivalent ratios.

Miles	Feet
0	0
1	5,280
2	?
3	?
?	21,120

> **Comparing ratios numerically.** Students might explore several tables of values describing equivalent ratios to compare them. For example, the two tables below describe library fines per day charged by two libraries. Students should be able to determine which library charges more per day either by looking at the unit rate when the number of days overdue is 1 or by observing the growth factor in each table.

Library A		Library B	
Days overdue	Total fine	Days overdue	Total fine
0	0	0	0
1	$0.50	1	$0.20
2	$1.00	2	$0.40
3	$1.50	3	$0.60
4	$2.00	4	$0.80

When relationships describe one variable as a multiple of another, the rate of growth in a table of values in which the independent variable increases by 1 each time is, in fact, the unit rate.

Good Questions to Ask

* Ask students to describe the relationship between inches and feet in at least three different ways. [**Answer (example):** 1 foot = 12 inches, 1 inch = $\frac{1}{12}$ foot, 2 feet = 24 inches.]
* Provide a table of values showing a proportional relationship, for example, number of legs for a given number of cows or number of eggs in a given number of egg cartons. Provide some of the data but not all, and ask students to first determine the missing pieces and then plot the data from the table as ordered pairs on a coordinate grid. Have the students describe the plot. [**Answer:** The plot should be a line through the origin.]
* Ask students to describe a variety of non-unit-rate situations using unit rates, for example, 3 grapefruit for $1.99 as 1 grapefruit for $0.67.

- Ask students to create a table of values showing equivalent ratios or rates that grow much more quickly than those in the table given below. Then ask for a table of values showing equivalent ratios or rates that grow slightly less quickly.

Feet	Inches
1	12
2	24
3	36
4	48
5	60

[*Answer (example)*: A table relating yards to inches could be provided as one growing more quickly, and a table describing the number of toes for different numbers of people could be an example of one growing slightly less quickly.]

Using a Coordinate Grid to Visualize Algebraic Relationships

The Number System	CCSSM 6.NS
Apply and extend previous understandings of numbers to the system of rational numbers.	

8. Solve real-world and mathematical problems by graphing points in all four quadrants of the coordinate plane. Include use of coordinates and absolute value to find distances between points with the same first coordinate or the same second coordinate.

IMPORTANT UNDERLYING IDEAS

> *Representing distances on a coordinate plane.* Students can use their knowledge of operations with integers or rational numbers to determine the distance between points with the same first or last coordinate on a coordinate grid. For example, the distance between $(-1,3)$ and $(4,3) = 4 - (-1) = 5$, or the distance between $(-2,4)$ and $(-2,-2) = 4 - (-2) = 6$.

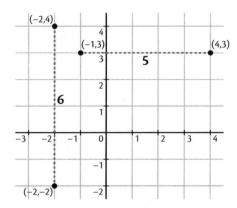

We want students to realize, more generally, that the undirected distance between (a,b) and $(a,c) = b - c$, or $c - b$, whichever is positive. Similarly, the undirected distance between (a,b) and $(c,b) = a - c$, or $c - a$, whichever is positive. If students are specifically instructed as to which is the starting point and which the ending point, a directed distance can be determined. Students should associate going right or up as moving in a positive direction and going down or left as moving in a negative direction. In the situation plotted above, the directed distance from $(-2,-2)$ to $(-2,4)$ is $+6$, but the directed distance from $(-2,4)$ to $(-2,-2)$ is -6.

> **Representing problems on a coordinate plane.** Problems that are suitable for graphing in all four quadrants of the coordinate plane are introduced at the 6th-grade level. The purpose of the graph is to display relationships between two variables described in the problem, as well as to serve as a tool to solve the problem. Simple linear relationships are the most likely ones to be explored at this level.

Often, tables of values are created to describe specific instances of the relationship, those tables of values are then used to plot some points, and a broader relationship is extrapolated and used. For example, to show the relationship between Fahrenheit and Celsius temperatures, students might create a table that pairs different Fahrenheit temperatures with the corresponding Celsius temperatures (rounded to the nearest whole degree) and then plot those points as ordered pairs, using the two values in each row of the table as the coordinates.

°F	°C
0	−18
10	−12
20	−7
30	−1
40	4
50	10
60	16

Students need to learn that they have choices about which variable to put in which column, but that the choice affects the look of the graph.

Once the points are plotted, students will likely notice the "linear" pattern. They can then use that pattern to extrapolate or interpolate to determine additional specific values of one variable for particular values of the other variable.

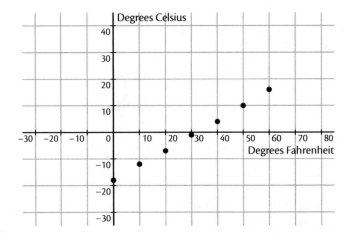

For example, students could use the graph above to estimate the Celsius temperature for 45°F as about 7°C or the Fahrenheit temperature for 0°C as 32°F.

Other real-world relationships involving negative numbers that students might graph involve the results when 10 is subtracted from double a number (i.e., $y = 2x - 10$), the amount of money more or less than $500 a person has in any particular month if he or she begins with $1,000 and withdraws $40 a month, or the distance between x and $-x$ on a number line. The latter case is shown below.

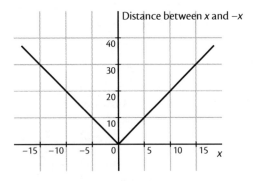

Many students are more comfortable using tables of values than graphs, but the graphical approach should be encouraged to allow students to become accustomed to it. Later, graphs will be particularly valuable and useful to students.

Good Questions to Ask

* Ask students to draw a horizontal line through Quadrants I and II. Then ask them to identify two points, one in Quadrant I and one in Quadrant II, that are exactly 10 units apart. [**Answer (example):** $(-4,3)$ and $(6,3)$.]
* Ask students to draw a vertical line through Quadrants I and IV. Then ask them to identify two points, one in Quadrant I and one in Quadrant IV, that are exactly 4.5 units apart. [**Answer (example):** $(4,0.5)$ and $(4,-4)$.]
* Ask students to consider the relationship between the amount of money more or less than $200 they have and the numbers of weeks of withdrawal if they start with $300 and withdraw $25 a week. Encourage them to create a table of values and plot some of the points to model the relationship. Then ask them to create and solve a problem using their graph. [**Answer (example):** If students plot the points $(0,100)$, $(1,75)$, $(2,50)$, they might graph points on the line $y = 100 - 25x$ and figure out that after 8 weeks, they would be $100 below the $200 mark.]
* Ask students to redraw the graph they created for the preceding question by reversing the order of columns in their table of values (i.e., reversing the values plotted as x and y). Have them decide whether a problem asking about the relationship can be solved using either graph and explain why. [**Answer:** Students should note that either graph can be used. For example, to decide how many weeks it would take them to get to $300 less than $200, they could start with the point $(0,100)$ and move right and down on the first graph to find the value x at the point $(x,-300)$ on the graph, or they could start with the point $(100,0)$ and move left and up on the second graph to find the value y at the point $(-300,y)$.]

Variables to Describe Generalizations

Expressions and Equations	CCSSM 6.EE
Apply and extend previous understandings of arithmetic to algebraic expressions.	

1. Write and evaluate numerical expressions involving whole-number exponents.
2. Write, read, and evaluate expressions in which letters stand for numbers.
   a. Write expressions that record operations with numbers and with letters standing for numbers. For example, express the calculation "Subtract y from 5" as $5 - y$.
   c. Evaluate expressions at specific values of their variables. Include expressions that arise from formulas used in real-world problems. Perform arithmetic operations, including those involving whole-number exponents, in the conventional order when there are no parentheses to specify a particular order (*Order of Operations*). For example, use the formulas $V = s^3$ and $A = 6s^2$ to find the volume and surface area of a cube with sides of length $s = \frac{1}{2}$.

IMPORTANT UNDERLYING IDEAS

➤ *Translating from natural language into algebraic expressions and equations.*
Since early grades, students have been translating from natural language into algebraic equations. Although they typically used symbols, rather than letters, in earlier grades, by 6th grade they have been using letters for some time. What students are less likely to be comfortable with is translating natural language into expressions. Many students are comfortable writing $3 + n = 10$ to ask what number to add to 3 to get to 10; fewer students are comfortable writing $3 + n$ to describe, more generally, the result of adding a number to 3.

Sometimes teachers familiarize students with some "key words" to assist them in translating from natural language into algebraic form, for example, suggesting that "groups of" becomes a multiplication sign or "shared" becomes a division sign. But that may not be enough and it may mislead. For example, the situation in which 30 more than an amount is shared by 4 might be translated as $30 + n \div 4$ instead of $(30 + n) \div 4$, or the situation where 36 is arranged into groups of 4 might, incorrectly, be written as 36×4.

A common error that students make is to mix up the algebraic expressions for the phrase "subtract a number from 10" and "subtract 10 from a number." This is viewed by some as an issue of order of operations, but in fact it is really an issue of the non-commutativity of subtraction. In one case, we start with 10 and then subtract the number n $(10 - n)$, and in the other we start with the number n and then subtract 10 $(n - 10)$.

➤ *Algebraic conventions.* Students must learn certain conventions that impact their comfort with writing and interpreting algebraic expressions. One is the fact that the multiplication sign is not used when a constant is multiplied by a variable, that is, rather than writing $3 \times n$, one would write $3n$. One reason relates to the fact that it could be unclear whether the multiplication sign is the variable x or a multiplication sign. It might be appropriate, when this convention is being discussed, to familiarize students with the term "coefficient."

Students must learn that one might write an expression such as $\frac{x}{4}$ or $x/4$ to mean $x \div 4$. This is unfamiliar to many students who have not yet recognized the relationship between fractions and division, that is, that $a \div b$ is $\frac{a}{b}$ or a/b, and vice versa. They also need to learn the meaning of an exponent, for example, that 3^5 means $3 \times 3 \times 3 \times 3 \times 3$ or b^2 means $b \times b$.

Yet another convention students must learn is how parentheses (or brackets) are used as a way to turn multiple terms into what is effectively a single term. For example, the expression $4(n + 3)$ is telling the reader to treat the $n + 3$ as a single entity. In fact, the order of operations rule that says that "one does what is in parentheses first" is based on the fact that the terms inside parentheses are being treated as a single entity. Students need to learn this. They also need to learn about "nesting" parentheses, that is, that one works from the inner parentheses outward. Applying this convention is the only way that they would know that they need to write "Start with a number. Add 3. Double that. Then subtract 5, and finally double the result." as $2[2(n + 3) - 5]$.

Another situation in which the importance of order of operations is apparent is in interpreting or evaluating an expression such as $3x^2 - 4$. This expression instructs the reader to square a number, then multiply by 3, and then subtract 4. This is quite different from instructions to first triple a number, then square it, and then subtract 4, which would be written $(3x)^2 - 4$.

> **Translating from algebraic expressions into natural language.** Just as it is important for students to go from natural language to algebra, it is equally important that students be able to interpret algebraic expressions in meaningful natural language. For example, consider the expression $3x + 8$. One way to view the expression is as shorthand for a set of instructions—"multiply a number by 3 and then add 8." The type of number x that is used is irrelevant. If, however, only integer substitutions are used, the expression could also be translated as "a number that is 8 more than a multiple of 3." This translation feels less like a set of instructions and more like a description of a type of number. Ideally, students should develop the ability to view the expression in either way, as appropriate.

Another example of an expression that can be interpreted in two ways is $30 - 2j$, which could be a set of instructions—"Choose a number, double it, and subtract it from 30"—or, if j is an integer, a description—"Numbers that are even," since every even number can be written in the form $30 - 2j$, for example, $2 = 30 - 2 \times 14$ or $20 = 30 - 2 \times 5$ or $40 = 30 - 2 \times (-5)$. Notice how reading the expression $30 - 2j$ as a set of instructions involves thinking holistically, not necessarily from left to right. A student could say "Start at 30 and then subtract double some amount," but somehow it feels more natural to start the description of the procedure with the amount j, which occurs at the end of the set of instructions.

It is useful for students to learn the word "term" to describe the separate components of an algebraic expression that are added together to make the expression. For example, $3j - 2$ has two terms, the $3j$ term and the -2 term, since this is really $3j$ added to -2. Notice that $3j$ is considered one term even though the 3 and j are combined through multiplication. This is disconcerting for some students; it seems odd to them that $j + 3$ is two terms, but $3j$ is only one.

> **Valuing the efficiency of variables.** Students should engage with the notion that algebraic symbolism is usually more efficient (in terms of length of expression

required) than natural language. Writing $2n - 4$ takes a lot less space than writing "Double a number and then subtract 4." This is one of the attractions of using variables.

But what students may not realize, but should be led to see, is that describing situations algebraically can actually make it easier to uncover new facts or relationships, as was discussed in the Introduction. For example, knowing that $3c + 4 = 6$ can lead students to other relationships through adding, subtracting, multiplying, or dividing the terms on both sides of the equation, for example, they can discover that $3c = 2$ or that $6c + 8 = 12$.

> **Substituting to evaluate expressions.** Students are sometimes given or sometimes generate algebraic expressions that must be evaluated for specific values of the variable. For example, students might be required to evaluate $40 - j^2$ for various values of j.

It is essential that students are confident with the order of operations conventions so that they will correctly evaluate expressions. For example, when $j = 10$, the expression $40 - j^2$ has the value of $40 - 100$, not $(40 - 10)^2$.

Substitution is an essential part of creating tables of values to uncover patterns. For example, by substituting different values for j, students might better understand why j^2 describes square numbers if j is an integer (substitution yields 0, 1, 4, 9, 16, . . . when using whole numbers) or that $2j + 1$ is a way to describe all odd integers if j is an integer (substitution yields 1, 3, 5, 7, . . . if positive whole numbers are used for j or $-1, -3, -5, -7, . . .$ if negative integers are used for j).

Students should always pay attention to what values are legitimate to substitute. For example, does it make sense for the variable to be a fraction or not, to be a negative number or not, etc.?

> **Algebraic expressions as generalizations.** Although many look at an expression such as $2n + 3$ as just something one substitutes numbers into, students should also look at an expression as a generalization, or statement of a general rule. In this particular case, no matter what number one begins with, the rule indicates that one should double that number and add 3. It is a way to describe an infinite set of numbers, all in one fell swoop. Similarly, the expression $3x^2 - 4$ describes an infinite set of numbers; no matter what number one has, one should square it, multiply it by 3, and then subtract 4.

Recognizing an algebraic expression as a generalization allows students to think of classes of numbers. For example, if n is an integer, writing the expression $3n - 5$ is another way of describing all numbers that happen to be 5 less than a multiple of 3, which also happens to be all numbers that are 2 less than a multiple of 3 (e.g., –17, –14, –11, –8, –5, –2, 1, 4, 7, . . .). Some algebraic expressions describe classes of numbers that are more familiar to students using other terminology, for example, numbers of the form $3n$, if n is an integer, are also called "multiples of 3." Numbers of the form $2n + 1$, if n is an integer, are also called "odd numbers."

➢ **Viewing an algebraic expression as a pattern rule.** It might be useful for students—particularly to connect with later learning about sequences and series—to recognize that an algebraic expression can be viewed as the rule for a pattern when positive integers are substituted for the variable.

For example, consider the pattern 2, 4, 6, 8, 10, . . . , which increases by 2 each time. Any term in the pattern can be calculating by multiplying the term position by 2. For example, the 15th number in the pattern is 2×15 (or 30). Therefore, the general rule for this pattern is that the nth term is $2n$. Looking at this in the opposite way, the algebraic expression $2n$ can be associated with the pattern 2, 4, 6, 8, 10, . . . because it is that pattern's rule.

The expression $4j - 2$ can be associated with the pattern 2, 6, 10, 14, 18, . . . , the expression $j^2 + 8$ with the pattern 9, 12, 17, 24, . . . , and the expression $5j$ with the pattern 5, 10, 15, 20, ... Some students might notice that the $4j - 2$ pattern increases by 4 each time, the $5j$ pattern increases by 5 each time, and the pattern associated with $6k + 3$ (9, 15, 21, 27, . . .) increases by 6 each time; they might notice that the coefficient of the variable tells how the pattern increases when there is no power associated with the variable.

Good Questions to Ask

* Ask students: How are the algebraic expressions you would write for each pair alike and how are they different?

  ◆ Subtract 30 from double a number, as compared to double a number and then subtract 30.
  ◆ Multiply a number by 4 and add 3, as compared to add 3 to a number and then multiply by 4.
  ◆ Add 5 to triple a number, as compared to add 3 to 5 times a number.

  [**Answer (example):** The first two expressions are exactly the same. Both times one would write $2j - 30$. The next two translate to $4n + 3$ and $4(n + 3)$. They both involve multiplication and addition and 4 and 3, but the second expression is always 9 greater. For example, $4(2 + 3) = 20$, but $4 \times 2 + 3$ is only 11. The last two expressions are $3j + 5$, as compared to $5j + 3$, so both involve multiplying and adding, but in one case the multiplication is by 3 and 5 is then added, and in the other case the multiplication is by 5 and 3 is added.]

- Tell students to imagine they had translated an algebraic expression into everyday words and some of the words they used were "triple," "less," and "five." Ask what the expression might have been. Encourage them to think of a few possibilities. [**Answer (example):** $3n - 5$, $20 - 5(3n)$. The first one reads "five less than triple a number." The second one reads "five times triple a number less than 20."]
- Ask students whether they think it is a good idea to write $4k + 1 = 17$ instead of "If you add 1 to 4 times a number, you get 17." [**Answer (example):**

  - I think it's better to use algebra because it takes less space.
  - I think it's better to use words because then I know exactly what it means.
  - I think the equation is good because then you could solve it by doing the same thing to both sides.]

- Have students write an expression where each of these results would occur:

  - If you evaluate it when $n = 5$, you would get 30.
  - If you evaluate it when $n = 5$, you would get -3.
  - If you evaluate it when $n = 10$, you get less than if you evaluate it when $n = 5$.
  - If you evaluate it when $n = 10$, you get twice as much as when $n = 5$.

  [**Answer (example):**

  - $6n$ **OR** $4n + 10$
  - $n - 8$ **OR** $3n - 18$
  - $20 - n$ **OR** $\frac{2}{n}$
  - $3n$ **OR** $8n$.]

- Ask students to write a pattern that each algebraic expression describes: $4n - 2$, $6n + 1$, $3n^2$. [**Answer:** 2, 6, 10, 14, 18, . . . ; 7, 13, 19, 25, 31, . . . ; 3, 12, 27, 48, ...]
- Ask students how the possible values of $5n - 2$ would be different if n could only be a positive whole number than if n could be any fraction? [**Answer (example):** If n is a positive whole number, the only possible values are numbers that are 3 more than a multiple of 5, such as 3 or 8 or 13, so they are 5 apart. If n can be a fraction, one could get values such as 1 or 10 by just using the right fractions.]
- Ask students when they could interpret the expression $1 - 2n$ as the set of negative odd integers. [**Answer:** When only positive integers are substituted for n.]
- Ask students how they might use an algebraic expression to describe all multiples of 5. [**Answer (example):** $5n$ if n is an integer.]

Equivalent Expressions

Expressions and Equations	CCSSM 6.EE

*Apply and extend previous understandings of arithmetic
to algebraic expressions.*

3. Apply the properties of operations to generate equivalent expressions. For example, apply the distributive property to the expression $3(2 + x)$ to produce the equivalent expression $6 + 3x$; apply the distributive property to the expression $24x + 18y$ to produce the equivalent expression $6(4x + 3y)$; apply properties of operations to $y + y + y$ to produce the equivalent expression $3y$.

4. Identify when two expressions are equivalent (i.e., when the two expressions name the same number regardless of which value is substituted into them). For example, the expressions $y + y + y$ and $3y$ are equivalent because they name the same number regardless of which number y stands for.

IMPORTANT UNDERLYING IDEAS

> *Using properties of operations to generate equivalent expressions.* Knowing the various properties of operations allows students to generate equivalent expressions. For example, because of the commutative property of addition, the expression $2j + 5$ is equivalent to the expression $5 + 2j$. Because of the associative property of multiplication, the expression $5(3c)$ is equivalent to the expression $15c$ (which is $(5 \times 3)c$). Because of the multiplication by one property, the expression $1 \times (4x)$ is equivalent to the expression $4x$. Because of the distributive property of multiplication over subtraction, the expression $5(x - 2)$ is equivalent to $5x - 10$. Sometimes the equivalent expressions involve fewer terms and sometimes not, as can be seen from these examples.

Often a number of properties are used to generate equivalent expressions. It can seem laborious for the student if each property must be cited each time it is used, but initially this process might be useful. For example, the reason that $(j + 4) + (2j + 5) = 3j + 9$ involves using a combination of the associative, distributive, and commutative properties:

- $(j + 4) + (2j + 5) = (j + 4) + (5 + 2j)$, using the commutative property,
- $(j + 4) + (5 + 2j) = j + (4 + (5 + 2j))$, using the associative property,
- $j + (4 + (5 + 2j)) = j + ((4 + 5) + 2j)$, which is $j + (9 + 2j)$, using the associative property,
- $j + (9 + 2j) = j + (2j + 9)$, using the commutative property,

- $j + (2j + 9) = (j + 2j) + 9$, using the associative property,
- $(j + 2j) + 9 = (1j + 2j) + 9 = (1 + 2)j + 9 = 3j + 9$, using the distributive property.

If two expressions are equivalent, when one is evaluated for a particular value of a variable, the result is exactly the same as when the other is evaluated for that same value for the variable, no matter what value is used. For example, $3j - 2$ is equivalent to $-2 + 3j$, so if $j = 0$, both are worth -2; if $j = 2$, both are worth 4; and if $j = 10$, both are worth 28.

> **Using models.** At some point, students might use concrete models to help them create equivalent expressions. For example, if one has 4 more than a number and 5 more than twice that number, one has a total of 9 more than the number added to twice that number, or 9 more than 3 of that number. So $(j + 4) + (2j + 5) = 3j + 9$. This could be modeled as shown below:

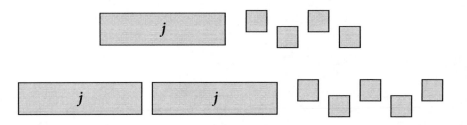

At this level, when student work with integers is limited, models might be best for only positive values of variables and constants.

> **Simplifying expressions.** When using properties to determine equivalent expressions involves reducing the number of terms, the term "simplifying" might be applied. For example, since $j + j$ is actually $1j + 1j = (1 + 1)j$, or $2j$, one might say that $j + j$ was simplified to $2j$; what was two terms became only one term.

Frequently students simplify expressions to have a clearer understanding of what those expressions really mean. For example, it is hard to recognize that $2m - 6 + 3(2m + 2)$ is actually just 8 times a number $(8m)$ until the expression has been simplified. It would take a lot more work to evaluate the expression in its first form than in the form $8m$.

Sometimes students simplify expressions to make it easier to solve equations. Using the equivalent expressions in the previous paragraph, one sees it would be much quicker to solve $8m = 64$ than to solve $2m - 6 + 3(2m + 2) = 64$.

Students should be led to see why they are simplifying and not just be told to simplify.

Using models can often help students to simplify, as shown in the preceding section, where $(j + 4) + (2j + 5)$ was simplified to $3j + 9$.

> **Testing for equivalence.** It is essential that students realize that two expressions are equivalent only if they lead to the same value when they are evaluated, no matter what value is used. For example, $3m + 2$ and $2m + 4$ have the same value if m happens to be 2, but since they do not have the same value in lots of other situations (e.g., if $m = 0$ or $m = 1$ or $m = \frac{1}{2}$, etc.), they cannot be equivalent.

Because all substitutions for a variable must result in equal values if expressions are to be judged equivalent, it is impossible to test whether two expressions are equivalent only by substitution. Reasoning about properties of operations must be used to test for equivalence. So, for example, $3m - 2$ is equivalent to $2m + (m - 2)$ not because they have the same value when $m = 0$ or 1 or 2 but because the associative property for addition says that $2m + (m - 2) = (2m + m) - 2$, which, using the distributive property, is $(2 + 1)m - 2$, or $3m - 2$. This is an example of the mathematical practice standard of reasoning abstractly.

Good Questions to Ask

* Ask students to generate a number of equivalent expressions for the given one, indicating what properties of operations they are using to generate those expressions.

$$3m + 8$$
$$5 - 4m$$
$$6m$$

[**Answer (example):**

  ◆ For the first expression, I could show that it is equivalent to $(2m + 3) + (m + 5)$. The associative property could make this $2m + (3 + (m + 5))$, and then the commutative property could make it $2m + ((m + 5) + 3))$. Using the associative property again makes it $2m + (m + 8)$ and then $(2m + m) + 8$, and then the distributive property makes it $(2 + 1)m + 8$, which is $3m + 8$.
  ◆ For the second expression, $3 + (2 - 4m)$ is equivalent, using the associative property of addition, by thinking of 5 as $3 + 2$.
  ◆ For the third expression, $5m + m$ is equivalent, using the distributive property.]

* Ask students to use algebra models to simplify expressions such as $(3 + 2j) + (5 + j)$.
  [**Answer (example):** I see $3j + 8$. That can be diagrammed as shown below.]

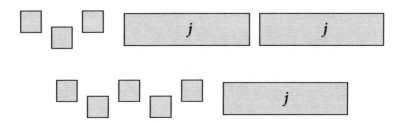

- Provide examples of expressions that can be simplified to exactly one term, without telling students that this is the case, then ask students what the simplifications have in common. For example, provide expressions such as $(c − 4) + (3c + 4)$ or $2m − 3 + 5m + 3$. [**Answer:** The two expressions simplify to $4c$ and $7m$. Both of these expressions have only one term.]
- Ask students to choose two equivalent expressions and show that their values are the same for at least five different values of the variable. [**Answer (example):** $3k + 2k$ and $5k$. When $k = 0$, I get $3 \times 0 + 2 \times 0 = 0 + 0 = 0$ and $5 \times 0 = 0$; when $k = 1$, I get $3 \times 1 + 2 \times 1 = 3 + 2 = 5$ and $5 \times 1 = 5$, etc.]
- Ask students to create two expressions that are not equivalent but are equal for at least some values of a variable. [**Answer (example):** $3k + 2k$ and $4k$ are equal when $k = 0$ but not when $k = 1$.]
- Ask students how they might prove that the expressions $2k + 3$ and $3k + 4$ are not equivalent. [**Answer (examples):**

  - I would substitute for $k = 0$ and see that they are not equal, so they are not equivalent.
  - I would model them and see that one model has 2 variable tiles and 3 number ones, but the other has 3 variable tiles, so they are not the same.
  - I would use properties to show that $3k + 4$ is actually $2k + 3$ added to $k + 1$. $2k + 3$ cannot be the same as $(2k + 3)$ and some more.]

- Request that students use the picture below to explain how each expression equivalently describes the area of the shaded shape.

$$3(n + 6) + 3n + 3(n + 6) + 3n$$
$$6(n + 6) + 6n$$
$$(n + 6)(n + 6) − n^2$$
$$4\left\{\frac{3[(n+6)+n]}{2}\right\}$$

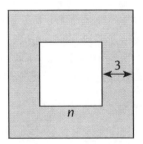

[**Answer (example):**

  - The first expression divides the shaded area into 4 rectangles—a rectangle across the top, which is 3 by $(n + 6)$; one at the middle right, which is $3 \times n$; one across the bottom, which is 3 by $(n + 6)$; and one at the middle left, which is $3 \times n$.

- The second expression pretends that the top and bottom rectangles are put together into a 6 by (n + 6) rectangle and the left and right ones are put together into a 6 by n rectangle.
- The third expression takes the length × width of the big square (i.e., its area) and subtracts the area of the inner white square.
- The last expression divides the gray area into 4 trapezoids with a short base from a side of the white square and a long base from the side of the gray square and a height of 3.]

Equations and Inequalities Involving Rational Numbers

Expressions and Equations	CCSSM 6.EE
Reason about and solve one-variable equations and inequalities.	

5. Understand solving an equation or inequality as a process of answering a question: which values from a specified set, if any, make the equation or inequality true? Use substitution to determine whether a given number in a specified set makes an equation or inequality true.

6. Use variables to represent numbers and write expressions when solving a real-world or mathematical problem; understand that a variable can represent an unknown number, or, depending on the purpose at hand, any number in a specified set.

7. Solve real-world and mathematical problems by writing and solving equations of the form $x + p = q$ and $px = q$ for cases in which p, q, and x are all nonnegative rational numbers.

8. Write an inequality of the form $x > c$ or $x < c$ to represent a constraint or condition in a real-world or mathematical problem. Recognize that inequalities of the form $x > c$ or $x < c$ have infinitely many solutions; represent solutions of such inequalities on number line diagrams.

IMPORTANT UNDERLYING IDEAS

➢ **_Testing the potential solution of an equality or inequality._** Students need to learn that an equation or inequality is solved by a particular value when that particular value makes the equation or inequality true. For example, 4 is not a solution to $3j = 8$ since it is not true that $3 \times 4 = 8$. But $\frac{8}{3}$ is a solution, because $3 \times \frac{8}{3} = 8$. Similarly, 5 is not a solution of $t > 10$ since 5 is not greater than 10. However, 12 is a solution (and only one of many) of $t > 10$ since 12 is more than 10.

> **Representing real-life situations with simple equations.** At the 6th-grade level, students extend their previous work with modeling problems involving all four whole number operations with equations and solving those equations to work with modeling problems involving operations with fractions.

Such problems might include, for example:

- You exercise $\frac{2}{3}$ of an hour a day. How many days will it be before you have exercised $2\frac{1}{2}$ hours? This problem could be modeled by the equation $\frac{2}{3}d = \frac{5}{2}$.
- You had some lemonade. You added $2\frac{2}{3}$ cups of lemonade to it. Now you have $3\frac{1}{3}$ cups of lemonade. How much did you start with? This problem could be modeled by the equation $2\frac{2}{3} + l = 3\frac{1}{3}$.
- You had $3\frac{1}{2}$ pounds of meat. If it was packaged into packages of $\frac{3}{4}$ pound, how many packages did you get? This problem could be modeled by the equation $\frac{3}{4}x = 3\frac{1}{2}$.

> **Solving simple equations.** Students should recognize that the solution to $ax = b$, when a and b are fractions, is the fraction $b \div a$ and that the solution to $x + a = b$ is the fraction $b - a$. In order to solve these equations, skills with dividing fractions and subtracting fractions with unlike denominators must be in place.

Analogies to or relationships to equations involving whole numbers can help students solve equations with fractions. For example, confronted with the equation $\frac{2}{3}k = 4$, it might be useful for students to think about how they would solve $2k = 4$ and simply use an analogous process—division. Or they might realize that if $\frac{2}{3}k = 4$, then $3 \times \frac{2}{3}k$ would be 3×4. Since $3 \times \frac{2}{3} = 2$, the equation is really equivalent to the equation $2k = 12$.

Some students might benefit from using diagrams. The diagram below shows that $\frac{2}{3}k = 4$, so it is fairly clear that another $\frac{1}{3}k$ (to make a whole k) would be another 2; the total of $\frac{2}{3}k + \frac{1}{3}k$, which is k, must be 6.

> **Distinguishing between equations and inequalities.** Students are more familiar with using and solving equations than with using and solving inequalities. It takes some students a bit of time to recognize why inequalities always have an infinite number of solutions, even though equations do not. For example, if a problem suggests that the temperature on a particular day was 50°F and the temperature another day was less, the equation $t < 50$ would describe all the possible tempera-

tures for the other day. There is an infinite number of solutions, since there is an infinite number of numbers less than 50. These could be shown on a number line by darkening the entire number line less than 50. Often an open dot is marked at 50 to show that it is not included.

If the problem had stated that the temperature was not more than 50°F, then 50 could also be included and the dot would be filled.

Sometimes inequalities have a finite number of solutions, rather than an infinite number, if the solutions have to be, for example, only positive whole numbers or only positive decimal tenths or hundredths within a certain range. An example like this might be something like the following: Jason had $100. His brother had less money. How much might his brother have had? The inequality $b < 100$ can describe possible situations for the brother's amount of money, and there are many solutions (e.g., $0, $0.01, $0.02, $0.03, $0.04, . . . , $99, $99.01, $99.02, $99.03, . . . , $99.98, $99.99) but not an infinite number.

Good Questions to Ask

- Ask students: Janelle told her friend that 4 is a solution of the equation $\frac{3}{2}y = \frac{8}{3}$. Do you agree or disagree? Explain your reasons. This could be a good example of the mathematical practice standard of constructing viable arguments and critiquing the reasoning of others. [**Answer:** It is not, since $\frac{3}{2} \times 4 = \frac{12}{2}$, which is 6 and not $\frac{8}{3}$.]
- Ask students: Are there many solutions to $\frac{3}{4}j = \frac{5}{8}$? Explain why or why not. [**Answer (example):** No, there is only one number that you can multiply by $\frac{3}{4}$ to get $\frac{5}{8}$. That number is $\frac{5}{8} \div \frac{3}{4}$, which is $\frac{5}{6}$.]
- Ask students to create an equation of the form $j + a = b$, where a and b are fractions, that has a greater solution than the equation $j + \frac{2}{3} = \frac{9}{2}$. [**Answer (example):** $j + \frac{1}{3} = \frac{9}{2}$ OR $j + \frac{2}{3} = \frac{11}{2}$.]
- Ask students to create a story that would match each equation. Then they should solve the problem.

$$5j = \frac{10}{3}$$
$$\frac{2}{5}k = \frac{4}{5}$$

[**Answer (examples):** For the first equation, $\frac{10}{3}$ cups of juice were divided up equally into 5 glasses. How much juice was in each glass? For the second equation, Jane and her best friend live $\frac{2}{5}$ of a mile apart. Jane and her grandmother live $\frac{4}{5}$ of a mile apart. How many times as far away does Jane's grandmother live as her best friend?]

* Ask: How are the solutions alike and different for the each of the members of the following pairs of inequalities?

For $x < 10$ and $x \le 10$?

For $x < 10$ and $x < 5$?

For $x < 10$ and $x > 20$?

[**Answer (example):** There is only one extra solution for $x \le 10$, and it is the number 10. All of the solutions to $x < 5$ are automatically solutions to $x < 10$, but there are a lot more solutions for $x < 10$—all the numbers between 5 and 10, including 5. For the third pair, the solutions are totally different; nothing that is less than 10 is also more than 20.]

* Ask students: Which problem has more solutions? Why?

  * A pitcher held 250 mL. Another pitcher held less. How much might the second pitcher hold?
  * A school had 250 students. Another school had fewer students. How many students might the second school have?

[**Answer:** The first problem has more solutions because a solution could be any fraction of a milliliter below 250. For the second problem there are only 250 answers—0, 1, 2, 3, . . . , 249. A unit of measure can be divided; a student cannot.]

Representing Linear Relationships

Expressions and Equations	CCSSM 6.EE
Represent and analyze quantitative relationships between dependent and independent variables.	

9. Use variables to represent two quantities in a real-world problem that change in relationship to one another; write an equation to express one quantity, thought of as the dependent variable, in terms of the other quantity, thought of as the independent variable. Analyze the relationship between the dependent and independent variables using graphs and tables, and relate these to the equation. For example, in a problem involving motion at constant speed, list and graph ordered pairs of distances and times, and write the equation $d = 65t$ to represent the relationship between distance and time.

IMPORTANT UNDERLYING IDEAS

> *Distinguishing between dependent and independent variables.* Much of the math
students will learn in higher grades relates to functions in which one variable is
related to another. Relationships between variables are useful because they allow
one to figure out new information from given information. Initially, linear relationships are highlighted.

Normally, one thinks of one of the variables as affecting the other, although it
can be a matter of perspective. For example, considering the relationship $d = 50t$
to describe how many miles (d) one might go in t hours if traveling at 50 mph, we
usually think of the amount of time as what we control, the independent variable;
the independent variable affects the value of the variable based on it, the dependent variable.

In a scientific experiment it is often clearer which variable is being controlled
and which, therefore, is the independent variable. When looking at the equation
$d = 50t$, knowing either variable's value gives information about the other variable's
value. One is more likely to think of distance depending on time rather than time
depending on distance, but if one thinks about varying distance and determining
the required time to travel that distance, it is distance that is treated as the independent variable.

> *Expressing a linear relationship by using an equation.* At the 6th-grade level,
equations relating variables are fairly simple, for example, $a = kb$ or $a + k = b$ (in
both cases, k is a constant). In the first case, one variable is an exact multiple of
another; another way to express this is to say that the two variables are directly proportional. For example, if $\frac{2}{3}$ of a recipe were being made, the amount of ingredient
in the reduced recipe is exactly $\frac{2}{3}$ of the amount in the original recipe; the equation
might be $n = \frac{2}{3}o$. In the second case, a constant is added to one variable to get the
other. For example, if a bank increased all of its fees by $5, the new fee for any
transaction would be $5 more than the old fee; the equation would be $n = 5 + o$.

Each of these equations could be described a different way as well. For exam-
ple, $n = \frac{2}{3}o$ could be described as $o = \frac{3}{2}n$. The equation $n = 5 + o$ could be described
as $o = n - 5$.

Students need to attend to which variable is multiplied or added to when creating the equation to describe a story. For example, there is a well-known miscon-
ception, discussed in the Introduction, where students express the situation "There
is a professor for every 20 students." with the equation $p = 20s$ instead of $s = 20p$.
To see that first equation is incorrect, some students might need to substitute values, for example if there were 40 students, most students would realize there
should be two professors. But if we substitute $s = 40$ into $p = 20s$, the number of
professors would be 800.

> **Expressing a linear relationship by using tables and graphs.** Often students col-
lect data about two variables, record the data in tables, and then use the tables to
help them graph the data to see the relationship visually. For example, suppose the
data below describe how the variable h relates to the variable m.

h	m
1	60
2	120
3	180
4	240

The student might draw the graph below and notice that the relationship, should
the table of values continue in the same way, forms a line.

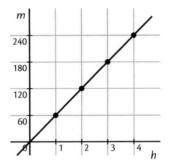

Good Questions to Ask

- Have students describe a situation in which one variable depends on another one.
  [**Answer (examples):** How much you pay for movie tickets depends on how many
  tickets you buy. How many days have passed depends on how many weeks have
  passed.]
- Remind students that the number of seconds that have passed is always 60 times
  the number of minutes. Then ask them to describe the relationship between the
  two variables—seconds and minutes—in two different ways. [**Answer (examples):**
  $s = 60m$ or $m = \frac{s}{60}$ or the table below.]

s	m
60	1
120	2
180	3
240	4

- Request that students create a table of values that would describe the relationship between h and c if $h = 25c$. Then they should graph the ordered pairs on a coordinate grid and tell what they notice. [**Answer (example):** I noticed that the pairs formed a line.]

c	h
1	25
2	50
3	75
4	100

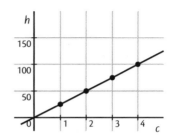

- Ask students what equation they would write to describe each situation:

   - The number of days is 7 times the number of weeks.
   - The number of heartbeats is 72 times per minute.
   - The download speed is 1.5 Mb per second.

   [**Answer (example):** For the first situation, $d = 7w$. In the second case, $h = 72m$. For the third situation, $a = 1.5t$.]

Solving Measurement Problems with Equations

Geometry	**CCSSM 6.G**
Solve real-world and mathematical problems involving area, surface area, and volume.	

2. Find the volume of a right rectangular prism with fractional edge lengths by packing it with unit cubes of the appropriate unit fraction edge lengths, and show that the volume is the same as would be found by multiplying the edge lengths of the prism. Apply the formulas $V = lwh$ and $V = bh$ to find volumes of right rectangular prisms with fractional edge lengths in the context of solving real-world and mathematical problems.

IMPORTANT UNDERLYING IDEAS

> ***Formulas for volumes of rectangular prisms.*** Essentially, measurement formulas are equations that relate different variables. We often substitute known values of certain variables to get unknown values of another variable.

For example, the formula $V = lwh$ is an equation that is true for any values of V, l, w, and h for a rectangular prism. If we know three of the values, we can use the equation to help us determine the fourth. If we know that a rectangular prism has a volume of $30\frac{1}{2}$ cubic inches, a width of $2\frac{1}{2}$ inches, and a height of $3\frac{1}{2}$ inches, we can deduce that $30\frac{1}{2} = l \times 8\frac{3}{4}$, so the length is $3\frac{17}{35}$ inches.

Students might solve multiplication or division questions involving volumes of rectangular prisms. They are likely to use multiplication when they know the linear dimensions or the area of the base and the height and want to find the volume. They are likely to use division when they know the volume and some of the linear or area of base dimensions and want the others. In 6th grade, the focus is on prisms with linear and area dimensions that are fractions rather than whole numbers.

Using measurement formulas is a very useful way to practice algebraic skills. It helps students not only to calculate measurements but also to see when equations are used, practice how they are solved, and recognize the difference between equations that state a relationship between variables and those in which the focus is solving for a missing value.

Good Questions to Ask

* Ask students for an equation to model this measurement problem: A rectangular prism has a volume of $20\frac{3}{4}$ in³. If the length and width are doubled, but the height remains the same, what is the volume of the new prism? [**Answer (example):** V (of the new large prism) $= 2 \times l \times 2 \times w \times h$. Since V (of the original small prism) $= l \times w \times h$, the large prism's volume is really $V = 2 \times 2 \times 20\frac{3}{4}$.]
* Tell students you used the equation $d = 24\frac{1}{2} \div 5$ to model a problem about the volume of a rectangular prism. Ask what the problem might have been. [**Answer (example):** A rectangular prism has a volume of $24\frac{1}{2}$ cubic units. If the height is 5 units, what is the area of the base?]
* Ask students to create a measurement problem involving the volume of a rectangular prism. Then ask them to create and solve an equation that would model the problem. [**Answer (example):** I built a rectangular prism whose height was half its width. If the length of the base was $4\frac{1}{2}$ inches and the volume was 100 cubic inches, what were the width and the height? *Equation:* $100 = 4\frac{1}{2} \times w \times \frac{1}{2} \times w$ or $100 = 2\frac{1}{4} \times w \times w$. The width is $6\frac{2}{3}$ inches and the height is $3\frac{1}{3}$ inches.]
* Ask students for the equation they could solve to determine the width of a rectangular prism that is very tall with a volume of $24\frac{1}{2}$ cubic units and explain the equation. [**Answer (example):** $24\frac{1}{2} = 20 \times l \times w$; I decided to use a height of 20 and a length of 2 inches, so the width was $\frac{49}{80}$ of an inch.]
* Ask students to explain why the formula for the volume of a rectangular prism involves three variables (length, width, and height) but the formula for the volume

of a cube can be stated using only one variable (side length). [**Answer (example):** When one has a prism that is not a cube, the length, width, and height could be different, so the volume formula has to consider all three of those values. But since a cube has a length and a width and a height that all have to be the same, once you know one of the values, you automatically know the others, so you don't need all three listed separately in the formula.]

Summary

By the end of Grade 6, students are able to translate fairly effectively between natural language descriptions of generalizations and algebraic expressions, and they can also view algebraic expressions as generalizations that describe sets of rules or sets of numbers. Students realize that algebraic expressions that appear different can be equivalent, describing the same generalization, and they realize that sometimes one form can be much simpler than another.

Students at this level can represent certain linear relationships with tables of values, graphs, and equations; can describe horizontal and vertical distances on a coordinate plane; and can solve simple linear equations with rational coefficients and/or constants. They can also use equations to solve simple measurement formulas involving volumes of rectangular prisms.

Recognizing Proportionality

Ratios and Proportional Relationships	CCSSM 7.RP

Analyze proportional relationships and use them to solve real-world and mathematical problems.

2. Recognize and represent proportional relationships between quantities.

   a. Decide whether two quantities are in a proportional relationship, e.g., by testing for equivalent ratios in a table or graphing on a coordinate plane and observing whether the graph is a straight line through the origin.

   b. Identify the constant of proportionality (unit rate) in tables, graphs, equations, diagrams, and verbal descriptions of proportional relationships.

   c. Represent proportional relationships by equations. For example, if total cost t is proportional to the number n of items purchased at a constant price p, the relationship between the total cost and the number of items can be expressed as $t = pn$.

   d. Explain what a point (x,y) on the graph of a proportional relationship means in terms of the situation, with special attention to the points $(0,0)$ and $(1,r)$ where r is the unit rate.

IMPORTANT UNDERLYING IDEAS

➤ *Recognizing proportionality using tables of values.* Students in earlier grades have met situations where unit rates are involved, for example, the number of minutes in a given number of hours (the unit rate is 1 hour = 60 minutes), the number of inches for a given number of centimeters (the unit rate is 1 inch = 2.54 cm), or the cost of different numbers of boxes of a particular cereal (the unit rate is cost of one box).

They have had experience creating tables of values describing the relationship between the two variables involved. For example, if a box of cereal costs $2.97, they might have created the table at the top of the next page to show the cost for different numbers of boxes of that cereal.

Number of boxes	Cost
0	$0
1	$2.97
2	$5.94
3	$8.91
4	$11.88
5	$14.85

When the table is created so that the value of the independent variable (in this case, the number of boxes) increases by 1, the dependent variable (in this case, the cost) increases by the unit rate. That makes sense because one more item results in one more unit. In 7th grade, the term "proportional" is introduced, and students learn that variables are proportional when a unit rate situation occurs. Students should notice that when the independent variable is 0, so is the dependent variable. If there are no boxes, there is no cost; if there are no hours, there are no minutes; if there are no centimeters, there are no inches.

Another way for students to test whether two variables are proportional is more indirect, but it is useful. If doubling the independent variable always doubles the dependent variable, the variables are also proportional.

> *Recognizing proportionality using graphs.* If students use a table of values as described above and graph each (independent variable, dependent variable) combination as an ordered pair, they will observe that the graph is always a straight line that goes through the point (0,0). Conversely, when they see such a graph, they should be able to create the related table of values.

If they observe a linear graph that does not go through (0,0), the two variables represented by x and y are not proportional. For example, consider the graph comparing Celsius temperatures to Fahrenheit temperatures (where 0°C matches 32°F).

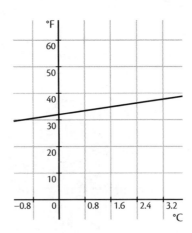

Even though temperatures on the two scales are not proportional, it is true that the Celsius temperature is proportional to a variable that represents 32 less than the Fahrenheit temperature.

The table below shows that °F is not proportional to °C, but °F – 32 is proportional to °C, since the values of that expression go up by a unit rate, specifically 1.8, and if the Celsius temperature is 0°, so is the Fahrenheit – 32 temperature.

Celsius	Fahrenheit	Fahrenheit – 32
0	32	0
1	33.8	1.8
2	35.6	3.6
3	37.4	5.4
4	39.2	7.2

Because a unit rate is always involved in proportional situations, students might observe that the y-value associated with the x-value of 1 is that unit rate. Thus the graph always goes through $(1,r)$, where r is the unit rate. For example, if one graphs the number of seconds in different numbers of hours, the graph goes through $(0,0)$, since 0 hours is also 0 seconds, but the graph also goes through $(1,3600)$ since there are 3600 seconds in 1 hour, that is, the unit rate. Students should notice that the increase in the y-coordinate for each increase of 1 in the x-coordinate anywhere in the graph is the unit rate.

> **Recognizing proportionality using equations.** Students, upon looking at a table of values showing a proportional relationship, should notice that the y-coordinate is always a multiple of the x-coordinate. The multiplier is the unit rate. For example, if one relates the number of people to the number of eyes those people have, the number of eyes is always double the number of people. This can be described in an equation as $e = 2p$. In the case of the cost of different numbers of boxes of cereal described earlier, the cost is 2.97 multiplied by the number of boxes. The equation would be $c = 2.97n$.

Students should notice that all of these equations are of the form $y = rx$, where x is the value of the independent variable, r is the unit rate, and y is the value of the associated dependent variable.

Good Questions to Ask

• Ask students why, if $y = 3x$, the following are true:

  ◆ y is proportional to x.
  ◆ If x is doubled, y is doubled.
  ◆ If x is tripled, y is tripled.

[*Answer (example):* *y* is proportional to *x* because if you create a table of values, 0 matches 0 and the increase when *x* increases by 1 is always 3. If *y* = 3(2*x*), then *y* = 6*x*, which is double 3*x*. If *y* = 3(3*x*), then *y* = 9*x*, which is triple 3*x*.]

- Ask students to indicate what variables *x* and *y* might represent if *y* = 4*x*. Then have them describe why it makes sense that those variables are proportional. [*Answer (example):* *x* could be the side length of a square and *y* could be the perimeter. It makes sense that when the side length increases by 1, the perimeter increases by exactly 4 every time.]
- Ask students why the variables represented by *x* and *y* in the graph shown below cannot be proportional. Then ask why the variables *x* and (*y* − 5) are proportional.

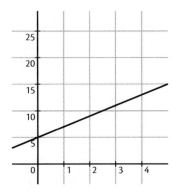

[*Answer (example):* They are not proportional since the graph does not go through (0,0) even though it is a line. If one decreased each *y*-coordinate by 5, then the graph would go through (0,0) and it would still be a line; the variables would then be proportional.]

- Ask students to describe several pairs of proportional variables. Have them prove why the pairs are correct. [*Answer (example):* The number of shoes and the number of pairs; these are proportional since the number of pairs is exactly half of the number of shoes, so the equation is *p* = 0.5*s*. Another example is the cost of different numbers of the same kind of candy bar since the price of the candy bar is a unit rate.]

Properties of Operations with Rational Numbers

The Number System	CCSSM 7.NS

Apply and extend previous understandings of operations with fractions to add, subtract, multiply, and divide rational numbers.

1. Apply and extend previous understandings of addition and subtraction to add and subtract rational numbers; represent addition and subtraction on a horizontal or vertical number line diagram.

   d. Apply properties of operations as strategies to add and subtract rational numbers.

2. Apply and extend previous understandings of multiplication and division and of fractions to multiply and divide rational numbers.

   a. Understand that multiplication is extended from fractions to rational numbers by requiring that operations continue to satisfy the properties of operations, particularly the distributive property, leading to products such as $(-1)(-1) = 1$ and the rules for multiplying signed numbers. Interpret products of rational numbers by describing real-world contexts.

   b. Understand that integers can be divided, provided that the divisor is not zero, and every quotient of integers (with non-zero divisor) is a rational number. If p and q are integers, then $-\left(\frac{p}{q}\right) = \frac{-p}{q} = \frac{p}{-q}$. Interpret quotients of rational numbers by describing real-world contexts.

   c. Apply properties of operations as strategies to multiply and divide rational numbers.

3. Solve real-world and mathematical problems involving the four operations with rational numbers.

IMPORTANT UNDERLYING IDEAS

> *Using number properties to define sums and differences involving negative numbers.* Students already know how to add positive numbers. They need to extend their repertoire to the ability to add two negatives or a positive and a negative.

Adding a negative number to another negative or a negative to a positive is often explained to students by using a contextual or a visual model. For example, if -1 is defined to be 1 less than 0, then it makes sense on a number line that $-1 + 1 = 0$ since if one starts at -1 and goes right 1, which is what $+1$ usually means, then one lands at 0.

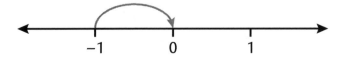

Similarly, if –1 represents the situation that someone owes another person $1, then paying that person $1 brings the debt to 0, so, again, –1 + 1 = 0.

Visual or contextual models can also be used to add values other than –1 and 1, but ultimately, it is valuable for students to see how the number properties make these results make sense, as described below.

The statement that –1 + 1 = 0, often referred to as the "zero principle," is the algebraic foundation, along with the number properties, for defining how addition with negative rational numbers works. For example, the expression –3 + 4 is equivalent to the expression –3 + (3 + 1). The associative property of addition tells us that this is the same as (–3 + 3) + 1. But (–3) + 3 is equivalent to 0 since it is –1 + –1 + –1 + 1 + 1 + 1, which, based on the commutative and associative properties of addition, is 0 + 0 + 0 = 0. That means that –3 + 4 = 0 + 1 = 1.

Students should come to realize that $-a = (-1)a$. This is based on the fact that since $1 + (-1) = 0$, then the distributive principle tells us that $a[1 + (-1)] = a + (-1)a = 0$; in other words, $(-1)a$ is what is added to a to get 0. But since $0 - a = -a$, it is also $-a$ that is added to a to get 0. Therefore, $-a = (-1)a$.

As a consequence of the fact that $-a = (-1)a$, we can add two negatives using the distributive principle. For example, $-4 + (-3) = (-1)4 + (-1)3 = (-1)(4 + 3) = -7$. More generally, $-a + (-b) = -(a + b)$, when a and b are positive.

Similarly, the number properties, along with the zero principle, define how subtraction works. The expression $-0.5 - (0.2)$ represents the value that must be added to 0.2 to get to –0.5. What must be added is –0.2 to get to 0, as well as another –0.5, that is, $-0.5 - (0.2) = -0.5 + (-0.2)$.

The expression $0.5 - (-0.2)$ represents the value that must be added to –0.2 to get to 0.5. What must be added is 0.2 to get to 0, and then another 0.5, which is why $0.5 - (-0.2) = 0.5 + 0.2$. More generally, $a - b = a + (-b)$, whether b is positive or negative.

> **Using number properties to define products and quotients involving negative numbers.** To multiply a positive number by a negative number, students can use a variety of visual models or they can use algebraic thinking. Although the models may seem easier for students as they acquire these skills, the models are in fact fundamentally built on algebraic principles. The algebraic approach is discussed here.

Using the fact that $-a = (-1)a$ and the associative and commutative properties for multiplication, it is clear that $a(-b) = a[(-1)b] = [(-1)a]b = (-1)ab = -ab$. That means that $3(-5) = -15$ and that $(-3)5 = -15$. It also means that $(-3)(-5) = -[3(-5)] = -(-15) = 15$. In other words, the fact that $-a = (-1)a$, along with the number properties, explains the rules for multiplying negative numbers.

The rules for dividing negative numbers fall out of the rules for multiplying negative numbers, since multiplication is division in reverse. For example, since negative × positive = negative, that means that negative ÷ positive = negative or negative ÷ negative = positive. Since negative × negative = positive, that means that positive ÷ negative = negative.

It is also important for students to realize that the rules for multiplying and dividing signed numbers explain why a fraction such as $\frac{-3}{4}$ is equivalent to $\frac{3}{-4}$ and also equivalent to $-\left(\frac{3}{4}\right)$.

Students can what they know about equivalent fractions to show that $\frac{-3}{4} = \frac{(-1)(-3)}{(-1)4} = \frac{3}{-4}$.

Knowing that $(-3) = (-1)3$, the student can think of $\frac{-3}{4}$ as $\frac{(-1)3}{4}$, which is $(-1)3 \div 4$. By definition, multiplying by 4 should lead to $(-1)3$, so if $4x = (-1)3$, then $x = -1\left(\frac{3}{4}\right) = -\left(\frac{3}{4}\right)$.

> **Modeling and solving problems involving rational numbers with equations.** Although students learn operations of addition, subtraction, multiplication, and division with rational numbers, they often do not know when to apply those operations. That is probably the most important thing for them to learn.

As students write equations to solve problems, it is useful if the equation closely matches the situation in the problem. For example, if the problem states that someone paid back $45.20 on a debt of $100.30, the student might write $-100.30 + 45.20 = \square$. But if the problem states that someone who had $150 in assets now has a debt of $40 and asks how much money he had paid out, the equation $150 - \square = -40$ makes sense.

If the problem inquires about how many losses of $4 would lead to a total loss of $96, the equation $-96 \div (-4) = \square$ would make sense. If the problem asks how 4 people might equally share a debt that is $142, a student might use the equation $(-142) \div 4 = \square$.

Good Questions to Ask

* Ask students why it makes sense that $-10 + 10 = 0$. [**Answer (example):** I would add $-1 + -1 + -1 + -1 + -1 + -1 + -1 + -1 + -1 + -1 + 1 + 1 + 1 + 1 + 1 + + 1 + 1 + 1 + 1 + 1$. Using the commutative and associative properties over and over, the result is $0 + 0 + 0 + 0 + 0 + 0 + 0 + 0 + 0 + 0 = 0$.]
* Ask students why $-8 = (-1)8$. [**Answer (example):** I would use the distributive principle with $-1 + 1 = 0$. I multiply $8(-1 + 1)$ to get $8(-1) + 8$. Since this is 0, $0 - 8 = 8(-1)$, but $0 - 8$ is also equal to -8, so the two expressions are equal.]
* Ask students to use number properties and the zero principle to explain why:

$$(-5) + 3 = -2$$
$$(-3) - (-2) = -1$$
$$(-4)(-3) = 12$$
$$\frac{-6}{9} = -\left(\frac{2}{3}\right)$$

[*Answer (example):*

- (−5) + 3 = [(−2) + (−3)] + 3. Use the associative property to rename this expression as (−2) + [(−3) + 3], which is −2 + 0 using the zero principle. The result is −2 using the zero property.
- (−3) − (−2) = x if x + (−2) = (−3) and the number to add is −1.
- (−4)(−3) = ((−1)4)(−3) since −4 = (−1)(4).
  ((−1)4)(−3) = (−1)(4(−3)) using the associative principle of multiplication.
  (−1)(−12) is the opposite of −12 since (−1)(−12) + (1)(−12) = (−1 + 1)12, or 0 using the distributive principle.
- $\frac{-6}{9}$ = (−6) ÷ 9. The number to multiply by 9 to get −6 is −$\left(\frac{6}{9}\right)$, which is −$\left(\frac{2}{3}\right)$.]

- Ask students to create problems to match these number sentences:

$$(-40) \div 8 = \square$$
$$(-13) + \square = -33$$

[*Answer (example):* I was allowed to pay off my debt of $40 in 8 payments. How much is each payment? The temperature was −13° and then fell to −33°. By how much did it fall?]

Equivalent Expressions

Expressions and Equations	**CCSSM 7.EE**
Use properties of operations to generate equivalent expressions.	

1. Apply properties of operations as strategies to add, subtract, factor, and expand linear expressions with rational coefficients.
2. Understand that rewriting an expression in different forms in a problem context can shed light on the problem and how the quantities in it are related. For example, a + 0.05a = 1.05a means that "increase by 5%" is the same as "multiply by 1.05."

IMPORTANT UNDERLYING IDEAS

> *Using properties of operations to create equivalents.* Students use properties of operations to add algebraic expressions. Often this is done intuitively, but there should be a few opportunities for them to realize, more explicitly, how number properties play into these equivalences. For example, to add 3n + 2 and 5n − 8, the commutative property, the associative property, and the distributive property are used:

$$3n + 2 + (5n - 8) = 3n + 2 + (-8 + 5n) \qquad \text{Commutative property}$$
$$= 3n + [2 + (-8 + 5n)] \qquad \text{Associative property}$$
$$= 3n + [(2 + -8) + 5n] \qquad \text{Associative property}$$
$$= 3n + (-6 + 5n)$$
$$= 3n + (5n - 6) \qquad \text{Commutative property}$$
$$= (3n + 5n) - 6 \qquad \text{Associative property}$$
$$= (3 + 5)n - 6 \qquad \text{Distributive property}$$
$$= 8n - 6$$

Similarly, students might subtract algebraic expressions by using these properties. For example, to show $6p + 4 - (2p + 1)$:

$$6p + 4 - (2p + 1) = (6p + 4) - 2p - 1 \qquad \text{Distributive property}$$
$$= [(6p + 4) - 2p] - 1 \qquad \text{Associative property}$$
$$= [6p + (4 - 2p)] - 1 \qquad \text{Associative property}$$
$$= [6p + (-2p + 4)] - 1 \qquad \text{Commutative property}$$
$$= [(6p + -2p) + 4] - 1 \qquad \text{Associative property}$$
$$= [(6 - 2)p + 4] - 1 \qquad \text{Distributive property}$$
$$= 4p + (4 - 1) \qquad \text{Associative property}$$
$$= 4p + 3$$

One of the most useful aspects of algebra is the ability to use it to describe generalizations easily. For example, writing $2n + 3n = 5n$, which can be thought of either as addition or as factoring $n(2 + 3)$, is a simple way to describe an instance of the distributive property and to say that whenever one adds double a number to triple that number, the result is five times that number.

There are a variety of generalizations that students at this level might use to simplify calculations. For example:

- To calculate 15% of a number, add 10% of it to half of that amount (or 5%). This is true because $0.15n = 0.1n + 0.05n$, based on the distributive principle, and $0.05 = \frac{1}{2}$ of 0.1.
- To calculate the sale price if the discount is 40%, you can calculate $\frac{3}{5}$ of the original amount. This is true because 40% of $n = 0.4n$ and $n - 0.4n = 0.6n$, based on the distributive property; finally, $0.6n = \frac{3}{5}n$.
- To add 15% tax to a given price, multiply the price by 1.15. This is true because 15% of $n = 0.15n$ and $n + 0.15n = 1.15n$, based on the distributive property.

It is not essential that students write out the properties algebraically when solving these types of simple problems, but it is important that they understand the underlying algebra. These are all examples of the mathematical practice standard of looking for and making use of structure.

Good Questions to Ask

* Ask students to rewrite each algebraic expression below in a different form and discuss some of the properties used to do it:

$$4p + 4 - 2p - 3$$
$$5n + 8 - (-n - 4)$$
$$3(5n + 2)$$
$$5n - 10 + 20m$$

[*Answer:* The first expression simplifies to $2p + 1$ using the distributive, associative, and commutative properties. The second expression is equivalent to $6n + 12$ using the distributive, associative, and commutative properties. The third expression simplifies to $15n + 6$ using the distributive property. The fourth expression may also be written as $5(n - 2 + 4m)$ using the distributive property.]

* To calculate 75% of a number, Katie says you can take $\frac{1}{4}$ of the number and subtract it from that number. Does that always work? Why or why not?
[*Answer:* Yes, it always works. That's because 75% is $\frac{3}{4}$ of a number, which is $\frac{1}{4}$ of the number taken away from the whole number.]

* How can you figure out the sale price of an item that is $\frac{1}{3}$ off in just one step?
[*Answer:* Take $\frac{2}{3}$ of the regular price.]

* How could you figure out 35% of a number if you were told how much 20% of it was? [*Answer (example):* You could take $\frac{1}{4}$ of 20% of it to figure out 5% of it and subtract that amount from double the 20%.]

* What does this equation tell you about calculating the price of something: $n + 0.08n = 1.08n$? [*Answer (example):* It tells how much to multiply a price by if you want to add in 8% tax.]

Using Algebra to Solve Problems

Expressions and Equations	CCSSM 7.EE
Solve real-life and mathematical problems using numerical and algebraic expressions and equations.	

4. Use variables to represent quantities in a real-world or mathematical problem, and construct simple equations and inequalities to solve problems by reasoning about the quantities.
   a. Solve word problems leading to equations of the form $px + q = r$ and $p(x + q) = r$, where p, q, and r are specific rational numbers. Solve equations of these forms fluently. Compare an algebraic solution to an arithmetic solution, identifying the sequence of the operations used in each approach. For example, the perimeter of a rectangle is 54 cm. Its length is 6 cm. What is its width?

> b. Solve word problems leading to inequalities of the form $px + q > r$ or $px + q < r$, where p, q, and r are specific rational numbers. Graph the solution set of the inequality and interpret it in the context of the problem. For example: As a salesperson, you are paid $50 per week plus $3 per sale. This week you want your pay to be at least $100. Write an inequality for the number of sales you need to make, and describe the solutions.

IMPORTANT UNDERLYING IDEAS

> ➤ *Modeling problems algebraically.* Many real-life problems can be described using linear relationships. These relationships always involve a term that is a multiple of one of the variables, and they may or may not include an initial value as well. For example, if you pay $200 to rent a hall and $30 per meal for each guest who comes to an event, then the total cost, in dollars, is 200 added to 30 multiplied by the number of guests. This can be described using the equation $C = 200 + 30g$. The 200 is called the initial value; it is constant and does not change based on a variable. On the other hand, the rest of the cost is related to a variable, the number of guests. Knowing the number of guests allows one to predict the cost.

The proportional component of the relationship can involve a whole number multiple or a fractional multiple of a variable and can involve a positive or negative amount. For example:

- *Adding a fractional multiple:* $F = \frac{9}{5}C + 32$ (or $32 + \frac{9}{5}C$) is a relationship relating Celsius temperature to Fahrenheit temperature.
- *Subtracting a fractional multiple:* $B = 400 - 2.5w$ could describe the relationship between the amount left in a bank account that began at $400 with $2.50 withdrawn each week to the number of withdrawal weeks.
- *Adding a whole number multiple:* $C = 200 + 30g$ could describe the situation relating the cost for a dinner to the number of guests if it costs $200 to rent the dining hall and $30 for each guest's meal.

Students should look at the equations they create to see if they make sense in the context of the problem. For example, in the equation describing the money in the savings account, $B = 400 - 2.5w$, as w increases, B decreases, This make sense since if there are more weeks, more money has been withdrawn, and less money is left. In the equation $F = \frac{9}{5}C + 32$, as C increases, so does F, and that makes sense since if it gets hotter, the temperature increases in both systems. Notice, too, that if $F = 32$, $C = 0$, as it is supposed to be, so the equation feels correct. Thinking about whether the equations make sense is an example of the mathematical practice standard of reasoning abstractly and quantitatively.

Notice that the equation $F = \frac{9}{5}C + 32$ can also be written as $F = \frac{9}{5}(C + \frac{160}{9})$ using the distributive property. Students need to recognize that both forms are correct. In fact, any equation that can be written as the sum of a linear term and a constant can be written in the form $a = k(bx + c)$, where x represents a variable to the first power and k, b, and c are constants. For example, $S = 500 - 20w$ can be written as $S = 20(-w + 25)$ or $C = 200 + 30g$ can be written as $C = 10(3g + 20)$.

Sometimes, rather than an equation, an inequality describes a situation. For example, suppose Abby has only $100 and wants to pay for a skirt for $20 and some shirts that each cost $15; she wants to know how many shirts she can afford. Solving the inequality $15s + 20 < 100$ for possible values of s will give her the answer.

Or suppose someone wants to know what Celsius temperatures are higher than 50°F, This would require solving the inequality $\frac{9}{5}C + 32 > 50$ for possible values of C.

> **Solving linear equations.** There are many methods students might use to solve linear equations. One of the most basic is guess and check. Students would make an educated guess about a possible solution, evaluate to see if they are correct, and adjust the guess based on the results of the test. For example, for the equation $3x - 4 = 25$, a good first guess might be 9, because $(3)(9)$ is close to 25. If $3x - 4$ is evaluated when $x = 9$, the result is 23, which is too low, so the student knows x should be more. Since the result should be 2 more, and an increase of 1 in x would result in 3 more, the solution must be $9\frac{2}{3}$. Notice that the guess and check method encourages estimation, which is a good to encourage in students no matter which method is ultimately used to find the exact answer.

Another method for solving linear equations is to use a balance. A student might draw a model like the one shown below, where the length of 25 is balanced against the length of $3x - 4$.

Looking at the model, it is clear that if 4 were added to 25 to make 29, that amount would match 3 sets of x, so each x must be $\frac{29}{3} = 9\frac{2}{3}$.

Students might, of course, also solve an equation by using opposite operations. For example, if $3x - 4 = 25$, that means that 4 was subtracted from some number to get 25; if 4 is added back, that will give the number that 4 was subtracted from, that is, $25 + 4$ (which is $3x - 4 + 4$) $= 3x$, so $29 = 3x$. This means that some number, x, was multiplied by 3 to get 29, so dividing by 3, the opposite operation, tells what number was multiplied by 3; in other words, $\frac{29}{3} = x$ (or $3x \div 3$).

Although the preceding description could also be shown only symbolically, as below, students will understand what is going on better if they think through *why* each step makes sense, as described on the previous page.

$$25 = 3x - 4$$
$$25 + 4 = 3x - 4 + 4$$
$$29 = 3x$$
$$29 \div 3 = (3x) \div 3$$
$$\frac{29}{3} = x$$

Notice that there is often more than one correct sequence of steps to solve an equation. For example, suppose a rectangle had a perimeter of 60 inches and a width of 4 inches, and an equation was used to determine the length. The equation might be $8 + 2l = 60$. This might be solved by first subtracting 8 from each side and then dividing by each term by 2 (i.e., $2l = 52$ and $l = 26$), or it might be solved by first dividing each term by 2 and then subtracting 4 from each side (i.e., $4 + l = 30$ and $l = 26$). Notice that in the latter case, each term, not just the $2l$ and 60, is divided by 2. This is another way of recognizing that the equation could have been written as $2(l + 4) = 2(30)$.

> **Solving simple linear inequalities.** Students should become aware that if an inequality of the form, for example, $2x + 8 < 30$ were being solved, there would be an infinite set of values that would make it true, and all of those values would be on one side of the value of x that makes $2x + 8 = 30$ on the number line. Since $(2)(11) + 8 = 30$, then any value of x less than 11 makes $2x + 8$ less than 30, and any value of x more than 11 makes $2x + 8$ more than 30. Students might see this by using tables of values or reasoning or graphs.

Table of values:

x	2x + 8
0	8
5	18
10	28
11	30
12	32
13	34

Reasoning: $2x + 8$ means twice a number and 8 more. If x is positive and gets bigger, twice x gets bigger and so does 8 more than twice x. So if $2 \times 11 + 8 = 30$, then if x is more than 11, $2x + 8$ is more than 30, and if x is less than 11, $2x + 8$ is less than 30.

Graph: If a graph of $y = 2x + 8$ is drawn and a horizontal line is drawn at the value of $y = 30$, one can see that the y is only less than 30 if x is less than 11.

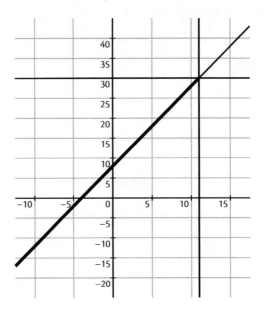

The solution set can also be graphed on the x-number line as all values to the left of $x = 11$, not including $x = 11$.

Students might solve the equation, instead of the inequality, and then test a number on either side of the inequality to see whether the solutions are greater than or less than the solution to the equality. For example, to solve $3c + \frac{1}{3} < \frac{4}{5}$, students might solve $3c + \frac{1}{3} = \frac{4}{5}$ to get $c = \frac{7}{45}$. Trying $c = 0$ gives a result of $\frac{1}{3}$, which is less than $\frac{4}{5}$, so it seems like the solution should be all numbers to the left of $c = \frac{7}{45}$ (like 0 is), so $c < \frac{7}{45}$. To be more secure, some students might test a greater value, for example, $c = 1$, to make sure that the greater values do not work. Notice that $3 + \frac{1}{3}$ is not less than $\frac{4}{5}$.

Some students will think that if the inequality is in the direction $ax + b < c$, then the solutions have to be in the form $x < d$, but this is not necessarily the case. For example, if $2x + 1 < 11$, it is true that $x < 5$. But if the inequality is $1 - 2x < 11$, the solution set is $x > -5$.

Good Questions to Ask

- What equations might you write to help solve each problem?
  - You had $100 in your bank account and put in $10.50 more each week. How long would it take to have $200 in the bank?
  - Jeff had $\frac{1}{2}$ as much money as his sister. But he got $30 for his birthday, and now he has $\frac{2}{3}$ as much as his sister. How much does his sister have?

  [*Answer (example):* $100 + 10.50w = 200; \frac{1}{2}s + 30 = \frac{2}{3}s$.]
- What problem might each equation or inequality help solve?

$$200 + 30p = 410$$
$$2(w + 40) = 120$$
$$\tfrac{2}{3}(s + 80) = 140$$
$$4x + 30 > 120$$

[*Answer (example):*

- There were 200 kids who walked to an event, and there were buses that each held 30 kids that brought more of them to the event. If there were 410 kids altogether, how many buses were used?
- The perimeter of a rectangle with a length of 40 inches is 120 inches. What is the width?
- A square 140" on a side is created by starting with another square, extending each side length by 80" and then taking $\frac{2}{3}$ of that amount. What was the side length of the original square?
- Jennifer needs to make sure she has more than $120 in her bank account to buy something she wants. She had $30 and has to earn the rest of the money in 4 weeks. How much money must she earn each week to meet her goal?]

- You solve a certain equation by first dividing by 4 and then subtracting 9. What might the equation have been? How do you know? [*Answer (example):* $4x + 36 = 100$. I know because, if I divided by 4, it was probably because all the constants or coefficients were multiples of 4 and the coefficient of the variable was 4. If I then subtracted 9, but that was after I divided by 4, I realize that the constant used to be 36. The 100 was a random choice; any other number could have been used instead.]
- Draw a diagram that would show why $4x + 25 = 53$ is solved by $x = 7$. [*Answer:* One possible diagram is shown below.]

53				
x	x	x	x	25

- A certain equation of the form $ax + b = c$ has the solution $x = \frac{3}{5}$. List four possible equations it could have been. [**Answer (example):** $5x = 3$; $10x - \frac{2}{5} = \frac{28}{5}$; $6x - \frac{3}{5} = 3$; $2x - \frac{1}{5} = 1$.]
- An inequality of the form $ax + b > c$ has the solution $x < \frac{3}{5}$. What might the inequality have been? [**Answer (example):** $6 - \frac{2}{3}x > 5\frac{3}{5}$.]
- How would you convince someone that the solution to the inequality $4x - 2 > \frac{4}{3}$ is $x > \frac{5}{6}$? [**Answer (example):** I would get them to solve $4x - 2 = \frac{4}{3}$ to get $x = \frac{5}{6}$ and then test to see that 0 does not solve the inequality, so they would know they should use values greater than $\frac{5}{6}$.]

Solving Measurement Problems with Equations

Geometry	CCSSM 7.G

Solve real-life and mathematical problems involving angle measure, area, surface area, and volume.

4. Know the formulas for the area and circumference of a circle and use them to solve problems; give an informal derivation of the relationship between the circumference and area of a circle.

5. Use facts about supplementary, complementary, vertical, and adjacent angles in a multi-step problem to write and solve simple equations for an unknown angle in a figure.

IMPORTANT UNDERLYING IDEAS

> *Formulas for circle measurements.* Essentially, measurement formulas are equations that relate different variables. For example, the formula $C = 2\pi r$ is an equation that is true for the values of C and r that pertain to any particular circle. If one knows either of the values, the equation can be used to help determine the other. For example, if a circumference is $6\frac{1}{2}"$, then the radius is known to be $6\frac{1}{2} \div 2\pi$, or slightly more than $1"$.

At the 7th-grade level, the formulas that might be considered include the following:

$$C = 2\pi r$$
$$C = \pi d$$
$$A = \pi r^2$$
$$A = \frac{\pi d^2}{4}$$

Using measurement formulas is a very useful way to practice algebraic skills. It helps students not only to calculate measurements but also to see how variables are related in realistic situations.

> **Solving angle problems.** When parallel lines are cut by a transversal, many angle relationships are created that can be described by equations. Equations to describe the picture below include these: $a + b = 180$, $c + d = 180$, $e + f = 180$, $g + h = 180$, $a + c = 180$, $c + e = 180$, $e + g = 180$, $b + d = 180$, $d + f = 180$, and $f + h = 180$.

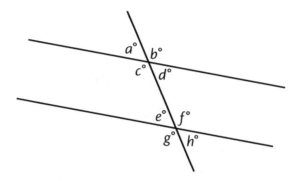

Students can use equations to solve for some values when they know others.

Similarly, if they know that two angles are complementary, students can use an equation of the form $a + b = 90$.

Good Questions to Ask

* Ask students for an equation or equations to model this measurement problem: The radius of a circle is doubled. What happens to the area? [**Answer (example):** The area of the small circle is $A = \pi r^2$. The area of the big circle is $A = \pi(2r)^2 = 4\pi r^2$. The area became 4 times as large.]
* Ask students for an equation or equations to model this measurement problem: The circumference of a circle increased by 10 cm. What happens to the diameter? [**Answer (example):** The circumference of a circle is $C = \pi d$. That means that $C + 10 = \pi d + 10 = \pi(d + \frac{10}{\pi})$. So the diameter increased by about 3, since it's $\frac{10}{\pi}$ greater.]
* Ask students to create a measurement problem involving the circumference of a circle. Then ask them to create and solve an equation that would model the problem. [**Answer (example):** A circular patio required 30 feet of fencing to enclose it. How wide was the patio? *Equation:* $30 = \pi d$. The answer is 9.55 feet.]
* Ask students how to write the formula for the area of a circle in terms of its circumference and why their answer works. [**Answer (example):** Since the radius is the circumference divided by 2π, you can just put those values in the usual area formula. $A = \pi(\frac{C}{2\pi})^2$.]

• Two parallel lines are cut by a transversal One of the angles is 105°. Draw a picture to show what the whole situation might look like. Are any of the angles supplementary to the 105° one? Are any complementary? What equation would you use to solve for the measure of the supplementary or complementary angle? [*Answer (example):* The picture might look like the one shown below. The equation $105 + d = 180$ would work to determine the size of angle d or angle a. There will be many supplementary angles to which students can point, for example, a and 105°. There are no angles that complementary to 105° because complementary angles total to 90° only.]

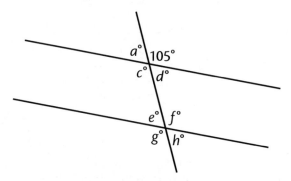

Summary

By the end of Grade 7, students are able to use properties of operations to calculate sums, differences, products, and quotients involving negative numbers and to create equivalent numerical expressions. They can use number properties to add and subtract algebraic expressions and can test for proportionality. They can model problems involving linear situations with either equations or inequalities, can solve those equations or inequalities using a variety of methods, and can use equations to describe relationships in circle and angle situations.

GRADE  8

Exponent Conventions and Properties

Work with radicals and integer exponents.

1. Know and apply the properties of integer exponents to generate equivalent numerical expressions. For example, $3^2 \times 3^{-5} = 3^{-3} = \frac{1}{3^3} = \frac{1}{27}$.
2. Use square root and cube root symbols to represent solutions to equations of the form $x^2 = p$ and $x^3 = p$, where p is a positive rational number. Evaluate square roots of small perfect squares and cube roots of small perfect cubes. Know that $\sqrt{2}$ is irrational.

IMPORTANT UNDERLYING IDEAS

> **Exponent conventions.** Students at the 8th-grade level learn that a^{-b} is another name for $\frac{1}{a^b}$. The explanation for this equivalence can be built on patterns. Students might note that in the table below, each time the value of the power goes down by 1, the value of the previous power is divided by the value of the base, in this case by 3.

Power	Value
3^4	$3 \times 3 \times 3 \times 3 = 81$
3^3	$3 \times 3 \times 3 = 27$
3^2	$3 \times 3 = 9$
3^1	3
3^0	
3^{-1}	
3^{-2}	

So 3^0 should be $\frac{3}{3} = 1$ and 3^{-1} should be $\frac{1}{3}$ and 3^{-2} should be $\frac{1}{3 \times 3} = \frac{1}{3^2}$. More generally, any base to the 0 power is 1 since we would be dividing that base by itself in a chart like the one above, any base to the -1 power is $\frac{1}{\text{base}}$, etc.

> **Exponent properties.** Students have met exponential notation before. It is at this level that they generalize rules for multiplying and dividing powers involving integer exponents. These generalizations are often expressed algebraically in these ways:

$$a^b \times a^c = a^{b+c}$$
$$a^b \div a^c = a^{b-c}$$
$$(a^b)^c = a^{bc}$$
$$a^b \times c^b = (ac)^b$$

The rules are explained based on the definition of exponents, conventions, and properties of numbers.

For example, $2^3 \times 2^5 = 2^8$ since 2^3 means $2 \times 2 \times 2$ and $2^5 = 2 \times 2 \times 2 \times 2 \times 2$, so $2^3 \times 2^5 = 2 \times 2 \times 2 \times 2 \times 2 \times 2 \times 2 \times 2$, which is 2^8. More generally, as long as the base is the same, multiplying a certain number of copies of that base by more copies of that base results in the total number of copies of that base.

The exponent law related to division of powers of the same base builds on the notion that $na \div nb = a \div b$. This makes sense by considering the equivalent fractions $\frac{na}{nb}$ and $\frac{a}{b}$ or by realizing that if $bx = a$, then $nbx = na$. Because $3^5 = 3^2 \times 3^3$, dividing both numerator and denominator of $\frac{3^5}{3^2}$ by 3^2 results in the remaining numerator factor of 3^3, so $3^5 \div 3^2 = 3^{(5-2)}$. This particular exponent law related to dividing powers of the same base also helps explain why $a^{-b} = \frac{1}{a^b}$, since $a^{-b} = a^{0-b} = a^0 \div a^b$, which is $\frac{1}{a^b}$.

The law related to a power of a power is based on the meanings of the powers. For example $(3^4)^2$ suggests that the product of 4 threes is multiplied by itself; as a result, there are 2×4 threes.

The law related to the product of two numbers to the same integer power is based on the commutative and associative properties of multiplication. For example, $4^3 \times 5^3 = 4 \times 4 \times 4 \times 5 \times 5 \times 5$ and that can be rearranged as $(4 \times 5) \times (4 \times 5) \times (4 \times 5)$, which is $(4 \times 5)^3$.

Good Questions to Ask

• Ask students to explain why each of the following is true:

$$3^4 \times 3^5 = 3^9$$
$$3^4 \times 4^4 = 12^4$$
$$(2^5)^2 = (2^2)^5$$
$$4^3 \div 4^8 = 4 \div 4^6$$

[*Answer (example):*

◆ If you multiply 4 threes by another 5 threes, there are 9 threes.
◆ $3 \times 3 \times 3 \times 3 \times 4 \times 4 \times 4 \times 4$ can be rearranged to be 4 groups of (3×4) multiplied together, and $3 \times 4 = 12$.

- If you multiply together 2 copies of 5 twos multiplied together, it's the same as multiplying together 5 copies of 2 twos multiplied together. There are 10 twos multiplied together either way.
- You can think of the division as a fraction and divide numerator and denominator by 4^2. What is left in the numerator is 4 and in the denominator is 4^6.]

* Ask students how exponent rules/laws can make the following calculations easier:

$$2^8 \times 5^8$$
$$20^3 \times \left(\tfrac{1}{2}\right)^3$$
$$2^8 \times 5^6$$

[*Answer (example)*:

- You could rename the first expression as 10^8, and that's just a 1 followed by 8 zeroes.
- You could rename the second expression as 10^3, and that's just a 1 followed by 3 zeroes.
- You could rename the third expression as $2^2 \times 2^6 \times 5^6$, and $2^6 \times 5^6 = 10^6$. That gives $2^2 \times 10^6$, which is 4×1 followed by 6 zeroes, which is 4 million.]

Equations of Lines

Expressions and Equations	**CCSSM 8.EE**
Understand the connections between proportional relationships, lines, and linear equations.	

5. Graph proportional relationships, interpreting the unit rate as the slope of the graph. Compare two different proportional relationships represented in different ways. For example, compare a distance-time graph to a distance-time equation to determine which of two moving objects has greater speed.

6. Use similar triangles to explain why the slope m is the same between any two distinct points on a non-vertical line in the coordinate plane; derive the equation $y = mx$ for a line through the origin and the equation $y = mx + b$ for a line intercepting the vertical axis at b.

IMPORTANT UNDERLYING IDEAS

> *Slope as describing unit rate.* Many of the relationships between variables that students explore at this level involve proportional relationships that can be "summarized" by describing a unit rate.

For example, the relationship $b = 72m$ might describe the number of heartbeats in m minutes. The unit rate of 72 heartbeats per minute is what makes that equation make sense. Similarly, the relationship $d = 365.25y$ describes the relationship between the number of years that have passed and the number of days that have passed (including the leap year factor). The unit rate of 365.25 days/year is what makes that equation make sense.

If these relationships are shown in tables of values, the unit rate appears in two ways. One way is the difference between successive values of the dependent variable (when the independent variable increases by 1). Another way is in the relationship between the independent and dependent variables in any row of the table; the dependent variable is always a multiple of the independent variable.

For $b = 72m$:

m	b
0	0 (0 × 72)
1	72 (1 × 72)
2	144 (2 × 72)
3	216 (3 × 72)
4	288 (4 × 72)

} 72

For $d = 365.25y$:

h	s
0	0 (0 × 365.25)
1	365.25 (1 × 365.25)
2	730.5 (2 × 365.25)
3	1,095.75 (3 × 365.25)
4	1,461 (4 × 365.25)

} 365.25

Sometimes, the unit rate reflects a decrease. For example, if the temperature begins at 0° and goes down 2° per hour, the relationship between hours and temperature is also proportional.

h	t
0	0° (0 × (−2))
1	−2° (1 × (−2))
2	−4° (2 × (−2))
3	−6° (3 × (−2))
4	−8° (4 × (−2))

} −2

When such relationships are graphed, they always go through the point (0,0) on the coordinate plane because the equation is always of the form $y = mx$ and if x is 0, so is y. But, more fundamentally, the graph goes through (0,0) since if there were, for example, no minutes or no hours, there would be no beats or no seconds.

When the relationships are graphed, because there is a unit rate, the value of the dependent variable at any point (x,y) is always the amount of the unit rate more (or less for a negative unit rate) than the value of the dependent variable y_1 at $(x - 1, y_1)$. For example, for the beats per minute situation, the number of beats in 4 minutes is 72 more than the number of beats in 3 minutes, or the number of beats in 10 minutes is 72 more than the number of beats in 9 minutes. Since slope is defined as the change in the dependent variable divided by the change in the independent variable, the slope is the unit rate $\div$ 1 = the unit rate.

For the heartbeat problem ($b = 72m$), the unit rate is 72, so the slope is 72. A graph of this relationship is shown below.

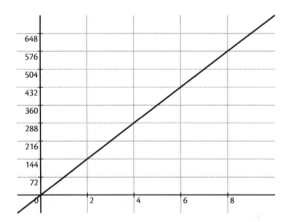

For the days in years problem ($d = 365.25y$), the unit rate is 365.25, so the slope is 365.25. For the temperature change problem ($t = -2h$), the unit rate is -2, so the slope is -2.

Students can compare the unit rates for different situations by comparing graphs and looking at slopes, by comparing tables and looking at successive increases, or by considering both approaches.

Students might be encouraged to look at triangles like those shown in the graph at the top of the next page for beats per minute and notice that the triangles showing the difference in the y-coordinate for a change of 2 in the x-coordinate are the same everywhere along the line.

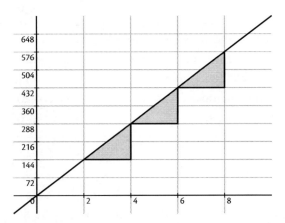

They might also be encouraged to notice that if different changes in the x-coordinate are used, the triangles are no longer congruent, but they are similar because the proportions are maintained.

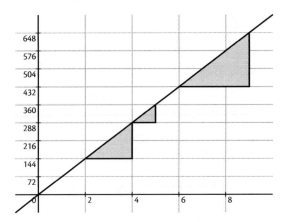

> **Formulas for equations of lines.** Although there are many ways to express the equations of lines, including in the form $Ax + By + C = 0$ (in which case the slope is $-A/B$), or the form $(y - y_1) = (y_2 - y_1)/(x_2 - x_1)(x - x_1)$ when the points (x_1,y_1) and (x_2,y_2) are points on the line, the focus in 8th grade is on expressing lines in what is called "slope-intercept form." This is because slope-intercept form often makes it easier for a student to predict what the line will look like.
>
> In slope-intercept form, any line is of the form $y = mx$, where m is the unit rate that expresses the slope, or $y = mx + b$, where m is still the unit rate that expresses the slope, but b is an initial constant value other than 0. For example, the cost of a membership at a gym that combines a $50 flat fee with a monthly rate of $20 per month could be described using the formula $C = 20m + 50$ or the equation of a line graph of the form $y = 20x + 50$. The 50 is the initial constant value and the slope of 20 is the unit rate, in this case the monthly rate. In this example, m and C are not proportional, although m and the variable that is $C - 50$ are proportional.

Notice that for the equation $y = mx + b$, when $x = 0$, $y = b$, so the line cuts through the y-axis at the point $(0,b)$, which is called the y-intercept.

Some students might wonder if $y = 3x - 2$ is a line, since they do not see a plus sign after the mx, but a minus sign instead. Students should be encouraged to explore these sorts of equations to see that these *are* lines, with intercepts below the x-axis, and that the equations could easily be rewritten in the form $y = mx + b$. For example, $y = 3x - 2$ can be rewritten as $y = 3x + (-2)$; the y-intercept is at point $(0,-2)$, 2 units below the x-axis.

Students should notice that there are no powers on the variables (other than the power 1, which is implicit when one writes x, which is x^1, or y, which is y^1) in the equation of a line. Two pieces of information fully determine the line: its slope and its y-intercept.

➤ *Relating linear graphs to linear equations.* With experimentation and using logical reasoning, students will discover that lines with a higher positive unit rate, or greater slope, are steeper than lines with a lower positive unit rate, if graphed with axes using the same scale. The value of the intercept is unrelated to the steepness. For example, comparing $y = 3x$ (dashed line) and $y = 5x$ (solid line) in the graph below, it is clear that $y = 5x$ is steeper.

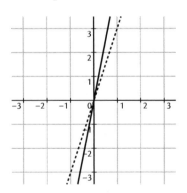

In the next graph (below), comparing $y = 5x$ (solid line) and $y = 5x + 2$ (dashed line), it is clear that the steepness is unaffected by the y-intercept.

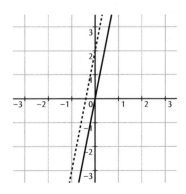

Students will also learn that a negative unit rate has the effect of creating lines that go from northwest to southeast (upper left to lower right) instead of southwest to northeast (lower left to upper right), that is, the y-values decrease as the x-values increase. For example, the graph below compares the lines for $y = -2x$ (dashed line) and $y = 2x$ (solid line).

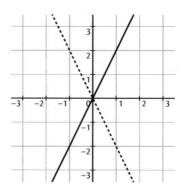

Students might be exposed to the effect of the scale on the axes on the steepness of the lines. For example, a line that should have a steep slope, such as $y = 10x$, could be made to look fairly flat with the right choice of scale on the axes. Both graphs below show $y = 10x$, but the steepness of the lines looks quite different because of the scale difference. The first graph goes up in increments of 5, whereas the second increases in increments of 100.

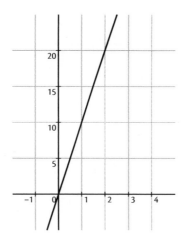
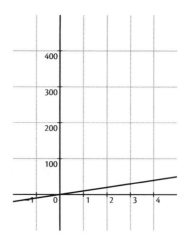

When given the equation of a line such as $y = 2x + 5$, the student should be able to graph it, most likely by starting at the intercept (0,5) and moving 1 to the right and 2 up (to reflect the slope of 2), plotting another point, joining them, and extending the line in each direction, as shown at the top of the next page.

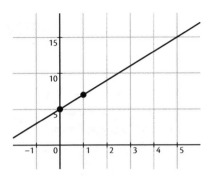

Another option for graphing a line is to plot two points. Students could substitute two different values for x, determine the corresponding y-values, plot those two points, and join them with a line. As shown below, for example, if $y = 2x + 5$, then if $x = 1$, $y = 7$ and if $x = 4$, $y = 13$. The points $(1,7)$ and $(4,13)$ could be joined. The two points chosen are arbitrary, and it is important for students to understand that; they could try various sets of two points and realize that they always get the same line.

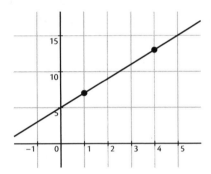

Yet another alternative is to choose two values for y, solve the equation to determine the corresponding values for x, and plot those points and join them. For example, if $y = 7$, then $2x + 5 = 7$, so $2x = 2$ and $x = 1$. One point on the line is thus $(1,7)$. If $y = 15$, then $2x + 5 = 15$, so $2x = 10$ and $x = 5$. Another point on the line is $(5,15)$. These points are plotted below. Again, the choice of the two y-values is arbitrary.

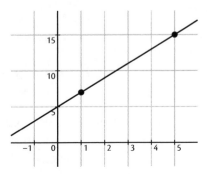

Good Questions to Ask

- Ask students to describe several situations, each involving a unit rate. Have them create tables of values to show where or how the unit rate appears in the table of values. [**Answer (example):** I would figure out the number of days in w weeks. The unit rate is 7, and it appears in the table (shown below) because it is how far apart the day values are when the week values are 1 apart.]

w	d
1	7
2	14
3	21
4	28

- Ask students to describe a realistic situation in which the unit rate might be 2 and to graph the associated line. Ask where the unit rate of 2 appears in the graph. [**Answer (example):** The number of nickels it would take to exchange for d dimes has a unit rate of 2. The graph is shown below. The slope is made apparent by using arrows—the y-value increases by 2 when the x-value increases by 1.]

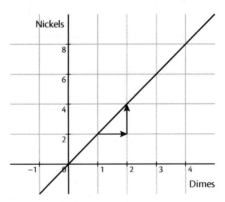

- Ask students to first predict and then test how the graphs for each pair of lines will be alike and how they will be different:

$$y = 2x \text{ and } y = 3x$$
$$y = 2x \text{ and } y = 2x + 3$$
$$y = 4x \text{ and } y = -4x$$
$$y = 2x \text{ and } y = -5x$$

[**Answer (example):**

- The $y = 3x$ line is steeper as long as you use the same scale on two different graphs or use the same coordinate grid. Both lines pass through the origin (0,0).
- The $y = 2x$ and $y = 2x + 3$ lines have the same slope but different y-intercepts.

- The $y = 4x$ and $y = -4x$ lines go in opposite directions, but they have the same degree of steepness when plotted with the same scale.
  - The $y = 2x$ and $y = -5x$ lines go in opposite directions, and the $y = -5x$ line is steeper as long as you use the same scale.]
- Ask students to create an equation for a steep line on a coordinate grid with the same scale on the x-axis as the y-axis where the y-intercept is -3. [**Answer (example):** $y = 6x - 3$.]
- Ask students how they would correctly graph $y = x$ so that the line looked somewhat flat. (This is an example of the mathematical practice standard of reasoning abstractly and quantitatively.) [**Answer (example):** I would make the scale on the y-axis different from the one on the x-axis by making the numbers go up much faster on the y-axis, as shown below.]

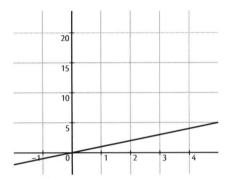

- Ask students what they are sure of and what they are less sure of about the equation of the line shown in the graph below. Acknowledge that there are no scales on the axes and explain that this was deliberate; students should not assume that 1 tick represents 1. (This is an example of the mathematical practice standard of constructing viable arguments.)

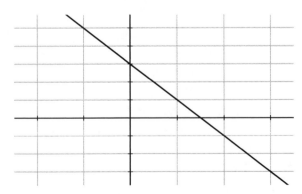

[**Answer (example):** The slope is negative, for sure, and the intercept is positive, for sure. But I can't be sure of the slope number or the intercept number without knowing the scale.]

Solving Linear Equations

Expressions and Equations	CCSSM 8.EE

Analyze and solve linear equations and pairs of simultaneous linear equations.

7. Solve linear equations in one variable.
   a. Give examples of linear equations in one variable with one solution, infinitely many solutions, or no solutions. Show which of these possibilities is the case by successively transforming the given equation into simpler forms, until an equivalent equation of the form $x = a$, $a = a$, or $a = b$ results (where a and b are different numbers).
   b. Solve linear equations with rational number coefficients, including equations whose solutions require expanding expressions using the distributive property and collecting like terms.

IMPORTANT UNDERLYING IDEAS

> *Different kinds of equations.* Although there are very different types of equations, many students never really notice or have their attention drawn to those differences. This can lead to great confusion for some students. For example, consider these four equations, all of which have a left side of $3x - 2$:

$$3x - 2 = 2x + 8$$
$$3x - 2 = 2x - 4 + x + 2$$
$$3x - 2 = 3x - 1$$
$$3x - 2 = y$$

The first equation is true for only one value of x, specifically $x = 10$. In this case, students might think of the x more as an unknown than as a variable, although technically, of course, the x can vary. In this case, it is just that other values of x do not make the equation true.

The second equation is true for any value of x since the expressions on either side of the equal sign are equivalent. Some students who do not understand the difference between types of equations struggle when they try to solve this equation using normal processes and end up with either an equation that says $3x - 2 = 3x - 2$ or an equation that says $0 = 0$ and do not know what to do at that point. They need to be alerted to the fact that some equations really are simply statements of equivalence and any value of x is a solution. This is indicated when the equation can be rewritten as $a = a$.

The third equation has no solutions; no value of x can make this true because the left-hand side will always be 1 less than the right hand-side. The two sides will never be equal. Many students are unaware that equations can have no solutions, having never been presented with this situation.

The fourth equation is clearly different because there is a second variable involved. Students should think of this equation as expressing a relationship between two variables. The single variable equation $3x - 2 = 10$ is actually a way of asking for what x-value the equation $3x - 2 = y$ has a y-value of 10. Students should realize that there are an infinite number of solutions to the fourth equation, just like there were for the second equation. But in the case of the fourth equation, not all values of x and y work, whereas in the second equation any value of x will work.

➤ **Processes for solving equations.** At the 8th-grade level, most students are more likely to use algebraic methods than guess and check or physical models to solve equations, but many students still need to use less formal methods to make sense of what they are doing. Because equations for Grade 8 students include those with rational coefficients and constants, it is important that students have good integer and fraction operation skills to be successful with this standard. Because these equations often involve determining equivalent expressions by simplifying, or require the use of arithmetic properties, it is useful that students hone these skills first, as well.

To solve, for example, $3(x - 4) = -8$, students need to know how to use the distributive property to expand $3(x - 4)$ as $3x - 12$, and they also need skills in working with integers.

Before students solve equations, they should be encouraged to estimate solutions so that they can judge whether the solution they get is even reasonable. For example, the solution to the equation $\frac{3}{4}x - \frac{2}{3} = \frac{5}{6}$ might be estimated in this way:

$\frac{2}{3}$ and $\frac{5}{6}$ are not that far apart, so the solution to the original equation might not be that far off the solution of $\frac{3}{4}x - \frac{5}{6} = \frac{5}{6}$. That would mean that $\frac{3}{4}x$ is the double of $\frac{5}{6}$, which is $\frac{10}{6}$ or about $1\frac{1}{2}$. If $\frac{3}{4}$ of something is $1\frac{1}{2}$, then the something is a bit more, so a good estimate for the solution might be 2.

In fact, the solution actually is 2.

One method to solve an equation such as $\frac{3}{5}x - 9 = 2\frac{1}{2}$ is by using a balance. This is an example of the mathematical practice standard of using appropriate tools strategically. First, the student might estimate to see that 10 is too small (since $\frac{3}{5}$ of 10 is about 6 and $6 - 9$ is negative), but 20 seems reasonable (since $\frac{3}{5}$ of 20 is about 12 and $12 - 9$ is close to $2\frac{1}{2}$). Knowing this, and realizing that $\frac{1}{5}x$ is about 4, they might draw something like the balance model shown on the next page, where $\frac{3}{5}$ of an x less 9 is matched to $2\frac{1}{2}$.

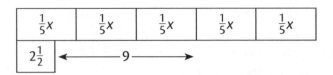

Looking at the model, it is clear that if 9 were added to $2\frac{1}{2}$ to make $11\frac{1}{2}$, it matches 3 sets of $\frac{1}{5}x$. That means $\frac{1}{3}$ of $11\frac{1}{2}$, which is $\frac{23}{6}$ (almost 4) is $\frac{1}{5}x$, and so $x = 5 \times \frac{23}{6} = \frac{115}{6}$, or $19\frac{1}{6}$.

As a teacher, one might be thinking, why doesn't the student just solve the problem algebraically? In effect, he or she is, but the visual model reinforces why the answer makes sense. Realizing that the whole thing is $19\frac{1}{6}$ is supported by the model for the equation and helps students make sense of what they have been doing. Using models like these also provides great opportunities for students to use the mathematical practice standard of critiquing each other's reasoning.

Physical models like these do not work as well if solutions are negative, since the quantity being shown as x needs to have a value greater than 0 in a length model.

Students might, of course, also solve the equation by using opposite operations. This works for equations with any type of solution, positive or negative. For example, if $\frac{3}{5}x - 9 = 2\frac{1}{2}$, that means that there is a value such that if 9 is taken away, only $2\frac{1}{2}$ is left. That value is clearly $9 + 2\frac{1}{2} = 11\frac{1}{2}$. But that $11\frac{1}{2}$ is only $\frac{3}{5}$ of the desired number, so the number x is obviously more than $11\frac{1}{2}$. If $\frac{3}{5}$ of that number is $11\frac{1}{2}$, then $\frac{1}{5}$ of that number is $11\frac{1}{2} \div 3$, and the entire number x is $(11\frac{1}{2} \div 3) \times 5$. Some students will realize that dividing by 3 and multiplying by 5 is, in effect, multiplying by $\frac{5}{3}$, or dividing by $\frac{3}{5}$.

The method described in the preceding paragraph is sometimes called the "cover-up" method, that is, it is almost like covering up $\frac{3}{5}x$ when realizing that $\square - 9 = 2\frac{1}{2}$ means that $\square = 11\frac{1}{2}$. This cover-up method is often successful for students (Arcavi, 1994).

So, algebraically, the steps in solving the equation were as follows:

$$\frac{3}{5}x - 9 = 2\frac{1}{2}$$
$$\frac{3}{5}x = 11\frac{1}{2} \qquad\qquad \text{(adding 9 to both sides)}$$
$$\frac{1}{5}x = 11\frac{1}{2} \div 3 \qquad \text{(dividing both sides by 3)}$$
$$x = (11\frac{1}{2} \div 3) \times 5 \qquad \text{(multiplying both sides by 5)}$$

The last two lines could have been shortcut into one line by dividing both sides of $\frac{3}{5}x = 11\frac{1}{2}$ by $\frac{3}{5}$.

Notice that there is often more than one correct sequence of steps to solve an equation, as seen above. When students are confronted with equations involving fractions, they often like to multiply both sides by a value that will allow them to get rid of the fractions first. So, for example, both sides of the equation $\frac{3}{5}x - 9 = 2\frac{1}{2}$ might be multiplied by 5×2, or 10, to get rid of both the fifths and the halves.

$$\frac{3}{5}x - 9 = 2\frac{1}{2}$$
$$6x - 90 = 25 \qquad \text{(multiplying ALL terms of both sides by 10)}$$
$$6x = 115 \qquad \text{(adding 90 to both sides)}$$
$$x = 115 \div 6 \qquad \text{(dividing both sides by 6)}$$

It is important to ensure that students multiply *all* terms (using the distributive property) by the value they have selected and not just multiply the values that initially include fractions. In the second step above, many students would forget to multiply the 9 by 10 to get 90 and leave it as 9.

Yet another way to solve a linear equation is to graph its line and look for the solution. For example, to solve $\frac{3}{5}x = 4$, one can graph $y = \frac{3}{5}x$ and look for the value of x that is associated with $y = 4$; another way to think about this is that students are looking for the place where the lines $y = 4$ and $y = \frac{3}{5}x$ cross. This is because this is the place (and the only place) where $\frac{3}{5}x$ actually is 4. At no other place is it 4. Notice, below, that this value is almost 7 (precisely, $6\frac{2}{3}$). The graph often is better for getting an estimate than an exact value, depending on whether or not the solution is easily visible using a particular scale.

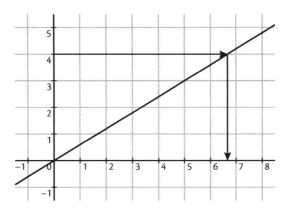

To solve the equation $3x + 5 = 2x - 5$, the students are looking for the place where the x-value in each graph leads to the same y-value. The reason is because if one substitutes an x-value on the left side of the equation and gets a particular value, the objective is to get the same value when that same value of x is substituted on the right side (or else the sides are not equal).

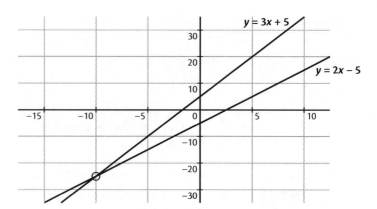

Notice that when $x = -10$, the y-values on both lines are equal, in this case $y = -25$, although the solution to the equation is the value $x = -10$ (there is no y in the equation). Notice that for *any* other x-value, either the left-hand side is worth more (one line is higher) or the right-hand side is worth more (the other line is higher).

Using a graph as suggested above for solving equations works well when the solution is either a whole number or perhaps halfway between two whole numbers; otherwise, it is more valuable to give an estimate than an exact answer. This approach to solving equations is also useful in preparing students for solving two equations in two unknowns.

Good Questions to Ask

* How are these equations alike? How are they different?

$$\tfrac{4}{3}x - 2 = \tfrac{5}{6}x$$

$$\tfrac{4}{3}x - 2 = (x + 1) + (\tfrac{x}{3} - 3)$$

[*Answer (examples):*

  * They are alike because they both have the same left side, but they are different because there is only one solution to the equation on top and a lot of solutions to the equation on the bottom.
  * They are alike because they both involve fractions and xs, and they are different because the bottom equation is more complicated.
  * They are alike because you can solve both of them, but one leads to the equation $x = 4$ and the other leads to the equation $0 = 0$.]

* Create an equation involving fractions that has only one solution. Then create an equation involving fractions with an infinite number of solutions. [*Answer (example):* $\tfrac{2}{3}x = \tfrac{5}{6}x + 2$ and $\tfrac{2}{3}x = \tfrac{1}{3}x + \tfrac{1}{3}x$.]
* Create an equation with no solutions. Why doesn't it have solutions? [*Answer (example):* $3x - 4 = 3x + 5$. This equation has no solutions because if you subtract $3x$ from both sides you end up with $-4 = 5$, which is not true.]

* How would you estimate the solution *before* solving each equation?

$$\tfrac{2}{3}x - 1\tfrac{1}{3} = 2\tfrac{1}{2}$$

$$\tfrac{2x}{3} + \tfrac{5}{3} = \tfrac{4x}{2} - 10x$$

[*Answer (examples)*:]

* For the first equation, I would think that this is really equivalent to $2x - 4 = 7\tfrac{1}{2}$ (by multiplying each term by 3), so that's close to $2x - 4 = 8$, so x is near 6. **OR** I would know that $\tfrac{2}{3}x$ is about 4 since $2\tfrac{1}{2} + 1\tfrac{1}{3}$ is close to 4, so x is about 6.
* For the second equation, I would think that $x = 0$ leads to $\tfrac{5}{3} = 0$, which is not true, so I'd try $x = 3$, and that leads to $3\tfrac{2}{3} = -24$; but $3\tfrac{2}{3}$ and -24 are farther apart than $\tfrac{5}{3}$ and 0, so then I'd try something closer to 0, such as $\tfrac{1}{2}$. If I let $x = \tfrac{1}{2}$, I get $2 = -4$, and 2 and -4 are pretty close, so I think the answer might be really close to $\tfrac{1}{2}$. **OR** I would think that this is actually $2x + 5 = -24x$ if I multiply through by 3; that can happen only if x is negative and pretty close to 0, or else $2x$ and $-24x$ would be very far apart, not just 5 apart. So, I think the solution is a negative number not far from 0, maybe near $-\tfrac{1}{4}$.]

* Describe two ways to solve the equation $\tfrac{5}{6}x - \tfrac{1}{4} = \tfrac{5}{8}x$. [*Answer (example)*: I could solve the equation algebraically, or I could use graphing. Two possible algebraic solutions are as follows:

  * I would multiply through by 24 to get rid of sixths, fourths, and eighths and end up with $20x - 6 = 15x$. Then I'd subtract $15x$ and add 6 to both sides to get $5x = 6$. Then I'd divide both sides by 5 to get $x = \tfrac{6}{5}$.
  * I would subtract $\tfrac{5}{8}x$ from both sides and add $\tfrac{1}{4}$ to both sides to get $\tfrac{5}{24}x = \tfrac{1}{4}$. Then I would divide both sides by $\tfrac{5}{24}$ to get $x = \tfrac{24}{20} = \tfrac{6}{5}$.

  For a graphing solution, I would graph the lines $y = \tfrac{5}{6}x - \tfrac{1}{4}$ and $y = \tfrac{5}{8}x$ and see where they cross. The x-value where the lines cross is the solution.]

Solving Two Equations in Two Unknowns

Expressions and Equations	CCSSM 8.EE

Analyze and solve linear equations and pairs of simultaneous linear equations.

8. Analyze and solve pairs of simultaneous linear equations.
   a. Understand that solutions to a system of two linear equations in two variables correspond to points of intersection of their graphs, because points of intersection satisfy both equations simultaneously.
   b. Solve systems of two linear equations in two variables algebraically, and estimate solutions by graphing the equations. Solve simple cases by inspection. For example, $3x + 2y = 5$ and $3x + 2y = 6$ have no solution because $3x + 2y$ cannot simultaneously be 5 and 6.
   c. Solve real-world and mathematical problems leading to two linear equations in two variables. For example, given coordinates for two pairs of points, determine whether the line through the first pair of points intersects the line through the second pair.

IMPORTANT UNDERLYING IDEAS

> *Relating systems of equations to real-life situations.* When teaching students about systems of two equations in two unknowns, the purpose of the exercise needs to be made clear. Students need to realize that, for example, a person might want to compare two possible situations involving linear relationships to see when one is preferable to the other or when one has the same effect as the other. This would be a common reason for considering the solutions of systems of two equations in two unknowns.

An example would be a problem such as "One gym charges a $100 membership fee plus $10 a month, and another charges a $40 membership fee plus $15 a month. Which is the best buy?" Some students might realize right away that, just as they learned that patterns that grow more quickly always surpass patterns that grow more slowly, the second plan will eventually be more costly, but the question could be about when that cut-off occurs, since initially the second plan is obviously less costly. The cost for the first gym could be described using the equation *cost* = $100 + 10m$, if m is the number of membership months, and the cost for the second gym using the equation *cost* = $40 + 15m$. Essentially, students want to determine the value of m where the cost values would be equal, realizing that for any smaller m, the second plan is better, and for any greater m, the first plan is better. Determining that value of m is, in essence, determining a common solution to the two equations.

Another type of situation in which two equations with two unknowns might be used is one involving mixtures. For example, suppose a vendor sells a certain type of snack for $10/pound and another type of snack for $8/pound. A question might be asked about the proportions in which the two snacks should be combined to form 20 pounds of a new snack that would sell at $8.50/pound and would lead to the same level of profit. Essentially, the goal is to find the correct values x and y so that $x + y = 20$ and $10x + 8y = 8.5 \times 20$, where x is the weight of the first type of snack and y is the weight of the second type of snack to be used in the mixture. The total weight must be 20, which is reflected in the first equation, but the cost proportions also need to be considered, which is reflected in the second equation.

A variation of this type of mixture problem might be something like this: "Ben drove a total of 300 miles. For part of that distance he averaged 60 mph, but for part of it he averaged only 40 mph. If the whole trip took 5 hours and 50 minutes, how much of it was at 60 mph and how much of it was at 40 mph?" Here the equations are

$$s + f = 300 \quad \text{and} \quad \frac{s}{60} + \frac{f}{40} = 5\tfrac{5}{6},$$

where s is the distance at 60 mph and f is the distance at 40 mph.

Yet another situation might be one like this: "3 jugs of orange juice and 1 jug of apple juice cost $15. But the price of orange juice increases by 20% and the price of apple juice increases by only 10%. The new total cost would be $17.70. What did each kind of juice originally cost?" This time the equations would be $3o + a = 15$ and $1.2(3o) + 1.1a = 17.70$.

What students should notice is that, in each of these situations, there are two variables and two relationships between them that must both hold true.

> **Interpreting a common solution numerically.** Students need to realize that for two equations to have a common solution, when the same values for x and y are substituted into each equation, both equations must hold true. This may seem simplistic, but not all students actually realize this, and explicit discussion of the concept might be valuable.

Consider the equations $x + y = 5$ and $x - y = 1$. To get the discussion going, the teacher might ask students to determine some values for x and y that will make the first equation true and then ask if those values make the second equation true. For example, if the student decided to let $x = 1$ in the first equation, then y would have to be 4 in order to make that equation true. But if $x = 1$ and $y = 4$ are used in the second equation, the second equation is not true, so $x = 1$ and $y = 4$ is not a common solution.

Students might be exposed to the notion that some pairs of equations have no common solution, for example, $x + y = 5$ and $2x + 2y = 12$, since if the second equation were true, $x + y$ would have to be 6 and not 5. It is impossible for the sum of two numbers to be both 5 and 6.

Students might also consider that there might be an infinite number of solutions, for example, for $x + y = 5$ and $2x + 2y = 10$, since both equations essentially say the same thing. Because the same information is repeated, any values that are true for the first equation, for example, $x = 1$ and $y = 4$, or $x = 20$ and $y = -15$, or $x = \frac{2}{3}$ and $y = 4\frac{1}{3}$, are true for both equations.

➤ *Interpreting and estimating a common solution graphically.* If students have experience solving single linear equations using graphs, as described earlier, it is not a big leap to solving two equations in two unknowns. In other words, solving the equation $3x + 5 = 2x + 12$, as described earlier, by graphing $y = 3x + 5$ and $y = 2x + 12$ and looking for the x-value where the two lines meet is, in effect, solving two equations in two unknowns where both equations have the same left-hand side, in this case y.

Students can extend this thinking. Imagine these two equations in two unknowns:

$$2y - 3x = 5 \quad \text{and} \quad 4x + 12y = 15$$

A student could solve each equation for y in terms of x and do what was discussed above. In this case:

$$y = \frac{3x}{2} + \frac{5}{2} \quad \text{and} \quad y = \frac{-x}{3} + \frac{5}{4}$$

$$\frac{3x}{2} + \frac{5}{2} = \frac{-x}{3} + \frac{5}{4}$$

But a student could also just draw the two graphs in the original form given, without first solving them both for y, and see where they cross, as shown below.

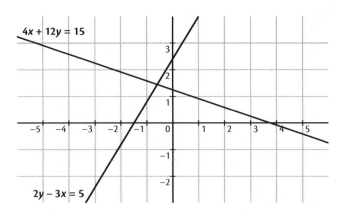

Each equation is solved by using the coordinates from any pair of points on that line. For example, two points on the line of $2y - 3x = 5$ are $(0,2\frac{1}{2})$ and $(1,4)$, so if $x = 0$ and $y = 2\frac{1}{2}$ or if $x = 1$ and $y = 4$, the first equation is solved. But notice that those two value pairs do not work for the line $4x + 12y = 15$. For that equation, if $x = 0$, y would be $1\frac{1}{4}$, so there is no common solution if $x = 0$. Similarly, there is no common solution if $x = 1$, since for the line $4x + 12y = 15$, when $x = 1$, then $y = \frac{11}{12}$, not 4 as for the other equation. Looking at the graph, the only time that the same x and y combination works for both equations is where the two lines cross, at about $x = -\frac{3}{4}$, where y is about $1\frac{1}{2}$. (In fact, solving the equations algebraically, the solution is $x = -\frac{15}{22}$ and $y = 1\frac{21}{44}$.)

Although it is obviously easier for students to start with equations whose graphs intersect at whole number values of x and y—for example, the equations $2x + 3y = 17$ and $7x - y = 2$ (which intersect at $x = 1$ and $y = 5$)—it is important for students to see how equations with more complicated solutions can still be estimated and to realize that the solution still appears at the intersection point of the lines.

Students could be more exact by using the following line of thinking: Suppose one line is $y = \frac{2}{3}x + 1$ and the other is $y = \frac{3}{4}x - 3$ (as shown below). At $x = 0$, the y-values are $1 - (-3) = 4$ apart. But the second line's slope is $\frac{1}{12}$ more than the first line's. That means that when x has increased by 12, the second line's y-value has increased by 1 more than the first line's, so at $x = 12$, the y-values are only 3 apart. The lines will intersect when the y-values are 0 apart, which would require 3 more steps of increases of 12 in x. Therefore, when $x = 48$, the lines should intersect. In fact, $\frac{2}{3} \times 48 + 1 = 33$ and $\frac{3}{4} \times 48 - 3 = 33$, so the lines do intersect at $x = 48$.

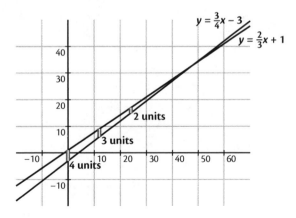

In other words, students could use information about how slopes differ and how intercepts differ to predict where two lines will intersect on a graph.

Students should also have experience with situations where the equations of the two lines have the same slope, but are not identical, in which case there are no common solutions, or situations where essentially the same line is described in two ways in the two equations, in which case there is an infinite number of common solutions.

For example, there are no common solutions to $2x + 3y = 5$ and $4x + 6y = 12$.

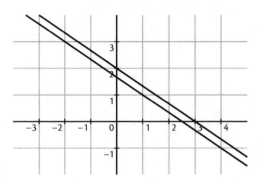

There is an infinite number of common solutions to $2x + 3y = 5$ and $4x + 6y = 10$, since they are the same line.

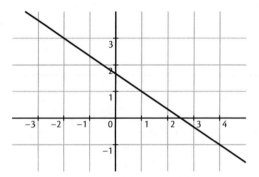

Once students learn to use graphing to estimate the common solution of two equations in two variables, they should start to see that the only possible results are either no solutions, an infinite number of solutions, or one solution. The first case occurs when the lines are parallel, the second case when the lines are identical, and the third case in all other situations. There can be only one solution if the lines are not parallel or identical since two points determine a line, and if there were two common points on two lines, the entire lines would have to be the same. Lines can only cross in 0, 1, or an infinite number of positions.

> ***Determining a common solution algebraically.*** Although a graph allows students to estimate common solutions for two equations in two unknowns, graphing is often not precise enough to give exact values. In this situation, or if the students prefer, the solution can be determined algebraically. Consideration of whether algebraic techniques are essential fits with the mathematical practice standard of attending to precision. Students should be expected to consider whether exact

solutions are required or whether estimates are sufficient in the context of the situation.

One common method for determining exact solutions algebraically is to rearrange both equations so that they share the same left-hand (or right-hand) side and then set the two other sides equal, since these two sides would have to be equal in order for there to be a common solution. In this way, an equation involving only one variable is created and students solve it using procedures they already know. Students need to understand that their goal is to end up with an equation with one variable, because they know how to solve that type of equation.

After solving this equation in one variable, they will know only one of the values, either x or y, for the common solution, but not both. They will have to go back to either one of the original equations to see what the relationship between x and y has to be, and then substitute the common solution value for the known variable to determine the common solution value for the still unknown variable. Students need to experience the fact that it does not matter which relationship they go back to; the results will be the same.

Shown below are two ways to determine a common solution for the equations $2x + 3y = 5$ and $2x - 3y = -12$, using the strategies described above.

If $2x + 3y = 5$, then $x = \dfrac{(-3y + 5)}{2}$

If $2x - 3y = -12$, then $x = \dfrac{(3y - 12)}{2}$

There is a common solution only if
$$\frac{(-3y + 5)}{2} = \frac{(3y - 12)}{2}$$
$$-3y + 5 = 3y - 12$$
$$17 = 6y$$
so
$$y = \frac{17}{6}$$
Since
$$x = \frac{(-3y + 5)}{2}$$
$$x = \frac{[(-3)(\frac{17}{6}) + 5]}{2}$$
$$x = -\frac{7}{4}$$

If $2x + 3y = 5$, then $y = \dfrac{(-2x + 5)}{3}$

If $2x - 3y = -12$, then $y = \dfrac{(2x + 12)}{3}$

There is a common solution only if
$$\frac{(-2x + 5)}{3} = \frac{(2x + 12)}{3}$$
$$-2x + 5 = 2x + 12$$
$$-7 = 4x$$
so
$$x = -\frac{7}{4}$$
Since
$$y = \frac{(-2x + 5)}{3}$$
$$y = \frac{[(-2)(-\frac{7}{4}) + 5]}{3}$$
$$y = \frac{17}{6}$$

Another approach students can take is the process called "substitution." The underlying idea, which needs to be discussed with students, again, is to use the information from both equations in such as way as to rearrange the given equations into one involving one variable, because students know how to handle this type of situation.

Using the same equations as were used earlier, $2x + 3y = 5$ and $2x - 3y = -12$, students might notice that they could use the first equation to realize that $2x$ must be equal to $-3y + 5$ in order for that equation to be true, and then they could substitute $-3y + 5$ for $2x$ in the second equation. What should be reinforced is that, by doing this, both relationships between x and y are being used simultaneously. In this case, the substitution would lead to $2x - 3y = -12$ becoming $(-3y + 5) - 3y = -12$, leading to $6y = 17$, just as was the case using the earlier method.

Alternatively, students could have realized that for the first equation to be true, $3y$ has to be equal to $(-2x + 5)$, and they could have substituted this into the second equation to get $2x - (-2x + 5) = -12$, which is $4x = -7$, just as was the case using the earlier method.

Students should learn that any substitution works, so they might look for a convenient one that does not require too much manipulation of the equations. This method, too, leads to the situation where only one variable in the common solution is known, and the value of the other variable must be determined by using one of the known relationships between the two variables.

Yet another algebraic method for solving two equations in two variables is called "elimination." This name clearly reminds students that the goal is to eliminate one variable in order to produce an equation that they already know how to solve; of course, the other methods, already discussed, have the same effect. However, in this case, students use equivalent equations which, when added or subtracted, result in the elimination of one of the variables. This is allowable because multiplying or dividing through an equation or adding equal amounts to equal amounts is legitimate in terms of the balance metaphor of what an equation means.

So, again, using the same pair of equations as before, $2x + 3y = 5$ and $2x - 3y = -12$, the student might notice that if the two equations are added, what is happening is that equal amounts are being added to both sides of the first equation, the amount being $2x - 3y$, but in the equivalent form of -12 when it is added on the right-hand side. The result, in this case, is the equation $4x = -7$, as before.

Had the equations been subtracted instead, so equal amounts are being taken from both sides of the first equation, the amount being $2x - 3y$, but in the equivalent form of -12 when it is subtracted on the right-hand side, the result is the equation $6y = 17$, as before.

There are times when the process is not quite as simple as in the example just shown, since the coefficients of x or y are neither equal nor opposites. In such cases, equations can be replaced by equivalent equations by multiplying through by factors to get to a situation where either the coefficients of x or the coefficients of y are equal and the equations can be subtracted to eliminate that variable, or where the coefficients are opposites and the equations can be added to eliminate that variable.

For example, consider the equations $3x - 2y = 12$ and $2x + 5y = 20$. Here, simply adding the equations or subtracting them would not eliminate a variable. But these equations might be solved by multiplying all of the terms of the first equation by 5 and all of the terms of the second equation by 2. In that way, the coefficients of y would become -10 and 10, and adding the equations would eliminate y:

$$3x - 2y = 12, \text{ multiplied by 5, becomes } 15x - 10y = 60$$
$$2x + 5y = 20, \text{ multiplied by 2, becomes } 4x + 10y = 40$$

Adding the two new equations results in the equation $19x = 100$, and a value for x has been determined. Going back to either equation to determine the corresponding value of y would be the next step.

Another option might have been to multiply the terms of the first equation by 2 and the terms of the second equation by 3, so that the coefficients of x would have become equal and the equations could have been subtracted:

$$3x - 2y = 12, \text{ multiplied by 2, becomes } 6x - 4y = 24$$
$$2x + 5y = 20, \text{ multiplied by 3, becomes } 6x + 15y = 60$$

Subtracting the two new equations results in the equation $-19y = -36$, and a value for y has been determined. Going back to either equation to determine the corresponding value of x would be the next step.

No matter which methods students use, it is critical that they understand that the goal is to use all the information given, but to transform that information first into an equation in one variable that they know how to solve, and then to go back again and use that information to get the value of the other variable to reach the common solution.

Good Questions to Ask

* Describe a problem involving the perimeter of a rectangle that could be solved by writing two linear equations in two unknowns. Tell what the equations are and why they are appropriate. [**Answer (example):** The perimeter of a rectangle is 80 cm. The length is triple the width. What are the length and the width? The equations are $2l + 2w = 80$ and $l = 3w$. Those equations are appropriate because I used the perimeter formula and the information that was given about the length and width.]
* Describe a problem that can be represented by writing two equations in two unknowns. Tell why those equations make sense. [**Answer (example):** There were 4 more boys than girls in a group of 34 kids. How many boys were there? How many girls? The equations would be $b + g = 34$ and $b = g + 4$. These equations summarize the two pieces of information provided—the total number of kids and the relationship between the number of boys and the number of girls.]

- Create two equations of lines that pass through (1,4). How do you know you are correct? How do you know there are other possibilities? [**Answer (example):** $3x + 2y = 11$ and $2x − 3y = −10$. I know I am right because I just wrote whatever left-hand side I wanted, substituted the value of 1 for x and 4 for y, and then wrote the number that was correct. I know there are other possibilities because I could have just chosen different left-hand sides.]

- Can you ever be certain of a solution of two equations in two unknowns that you find graphically or is it always an estimate? [**Answer (example):** I don't think you can ever be sure, because if a value is a fraction, it's really hard to tell exactly what fraction it is, and even if it looks like a whole number, it might be a fraction that is just really close to a whole number.]

- You graph to estimate the common solution of $y = 3x + 2$ and some other equation. The common solution is in Quadrant II. What might the equation be and what would your estimate for the common solution be? [**Answer (examples):**

  - $y = −x$. My estimate for the solution based on the graph would be $(−\frac{1}{2},\frac{1}{2})$. I tested and it was actually right.
  - $y = −\frac{1}{2}x$. My estimate for the solution based on the graph would be $(−\frac{5}{8},\frac{1}{3})$.]

- When you solve a pair of equations in two unknowns algebraically, why do you always seek an equation involving only one variable? [**Answer (example):** Because I know how to solve an equation involving one variable, or because there are too many solutions when there is an equation involving two variables and two unknowns and I had to find a way to have only one solution.]

- Describe a pair of equations in two unknowns you might solve using each method below and tell why you chose that pair.

  - By solving both equations for either x or y and then setting the two descriptions of that variable equal.
  - By substituting information from one equation into the other.
  - By using elimination and adding or subtracting the two equations.

  [**Answer (example):**

  - If the equations were $3y = 2x − 5$ and $2y = 7x + 2$, I might solve each of them for y, since that's an easy division, and then set the other two sides equal.
  - If the equations were $2x = 5y − 8$ and $3y + 2x = 20$, I might substitute the $5y − 8$ from the first equation into the $2x$ in the second equation since that would be quick and easy.
  - If the equations were $5x − 2y = 20$ and $6x + 2y = 30$, I would add the equations since adding $−2y$ and $2y$ gets rid of the ys.]

- How does looking at how far apart the slopes and intercepts are in $y = 5x − 4$ and $y = 10x − 12$ help explain where they intersect? [**Answer:** The y-values are 8 apart when $x = 0$ and the slopes are 5 apart, so when $x = 1$, the y-values will be only $8 − 5 = 3$ apart. To be 0 apart, you need to increase x by another $\frac{3}{5}$ of 5, so the lines intersect when $x = 1\frac{3}{5}$.]

Functions

Functions	CCSSM 8.F
Define, evaluate, and compare functions.	

1. Understand that a function is a rule that assigns to each input exactly one output. The graph of a function is the set of ordered pairs consisting of an input and the corresponding output.
2. Compare properties of two functions each represented in a different way (algebraically, graphically, numerically in tables, or by verbal descriptions). For example, given a linear function represented by a table of values and a linear function represented by an algebraic expression, determine which function has the greater rate of change.
3. Interpret the equation $y = mx + b$ as defining a linear function, whose graph is a straight line; give examples of functions that are not linear. For example, the function $A = s^2$ giving the area of a square as a function of its side length is not linear because its graph contains the points $(1,1)$, $(2,4)$ and $(3,9)$, which are not on a straight line.

IMPORTANT UNDERLYING IDEAS

> ➤ ***Defining a function.*** Functions are rules that relate a starting "position" called an input to an ending "position" called an output. For example, the rule could be "take a number and double it or take a number, add five, and then double it." What distinguishes a function from something called a "relation" is that there is only one output for a given input. This is not the case, for example, for the square root rule, where a number has two square roots, one positive and one negative.
>
> Notice that if a graph of a function is drawn, one way to test that it is a function and that there is only one output for a given input is the "vertical line test." If a vertical line is drawn at a point along the x-axis, it should hit the line for the function only once, not more times. For example, compare the graph of $y = x$, which is a function, with the graph of $y = \mathrm{sqrt}(x)$, which is not.

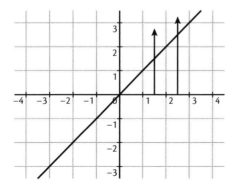
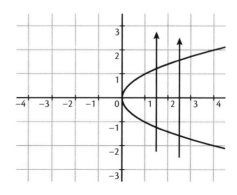

Although there can be only one output for a given input, there might be many inputs that lead to the same output. For example, if the function were the rule "the output is 1 if the number if positive, or –1 if the number is negative or 0," there is one output for each input but there are many inputs that lead to the output of 1 and many that lead to the output of –1.

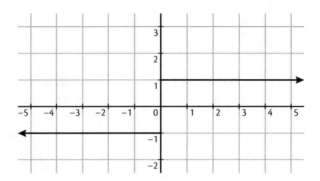

Students have been experiencing functions since early elementary years, but the relationships simply were not called "functions." For example, when students multiplied 3 by 4, they were considering the value of the function $3 \times \square$ when the input was 4. Or when they solved the equation $3 \times \square = 12$, they were considering the function $3 \times \square$ and determining when the output was 12. When students used the formula $P = 4 \times s$ to describe the perimeter of a square, they were using a function in which the input was the side length of a square and the output was the perimeter.

Other examples of experiencing functions might have been in student work with patterns. For example, suppose students were trying to determine the number of squares in the 20th picture of the pattern shown below:

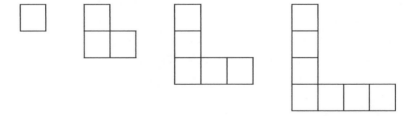

Students were, in essence, using the principle of generalizing to determine the function $f(x) = 2x - 1$ in order to predict the value of the function, defined only when x is a whole number, when x was 20.

Similarly, if they were attempting to determine the number of diagonals in an n-sided polygon, students might have used a pattern to help them notice that the number is $n(n - 3)/2$ and then justified this observation either geometrically or numerically.

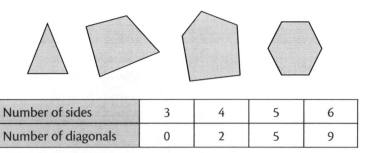

Number of sides	3	4	5	6
Number of diagonals	0	2	5	9

Sometimes students respond positively to the concept of a "function machine," a visual model where there is an input, a rule, and an output. They could be given any two of the three components and asked to determine the missing one. A function machine might be diagrammed something like this:

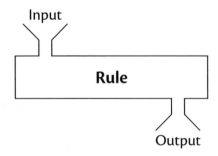

Notice that if the input and the rule are given, there is only one possible output. For example, if the input is 8 and the rule is "double the number and add 5," the output must be 21. If the output is 8 and the rule is "double the number and add 5," the input is determined by using reverse operations, that is, subtract 5 and take half, so in this case the input would be $\frac{3}{2}$. In effect, the equation $2x + 5 = 8$ was solved.

But if the input and output are given, students should realize there are many potential rules, for example, if the input is 8 and the output is 10, the rule could be "add 2" or it could be "double the number and subtract 6" or it could be "square the number, take half, and subtract 22." There is an infinite number of possible rules. Students should explore this phenomenon and apply the mathematical practice standard of making sense of problems and persevering in solving them.

Although many functions encountered by students at this level have inputs of single numbers, the input of a function could be something else, such as a pair of numbers, where the function rule is to add them.

Not all functions are numerical. For example, the function that has an input of a polygon and an output of its number of sides is familiar to students. A function could also have inputs of objects and outputs of the objects' colors, assuming each object has only one color.

> **Relating different representations of functions.** Functions can be represented verbally, numerically using tables of values, algebraically, or graphically. Each of these representations reveals information about the function.

For example, the verbal rule "double a number and add 5" reveals that the result is always more than double the number. The table of values below makes it very easy to see that if the input increases by 1, the output increases by 2.

Input	Output
1	7
2	9
3	11
4	13

The algebraic, or symbolic, representation of the function, often written $f(x) = 2x + 5$, tells us that the function involves the first power of a variable and no higher power and involves an initial value as well as a proportional relationship. This type of representation is also an efficient way to write the verbal rule. Sometimes, instead of $f(x) = 2x + 5$, one might simply write $y = 2x + 5$. Any other variables, not x or y, could also be used.

The graphical representation of the function shown below makes it clear that the function is linear.

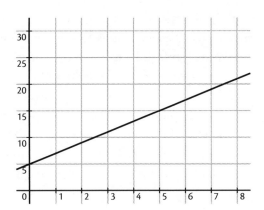

Notice that the graph is simply the set of ordered pairs that describe all possible input/output combinations. Because values of the input other than integers were used in the graphical representation (in contrast to the the table of values given above, which included integers only), a more complete picture of the function is presented with this type of representation than is possible with just a table of values.

➤ *Comparing functions.* Often functions are compared in terms of how fast they grow. Neither the verbal rule nor the algebraic representation makes the growth rate as plain to see as either a table of values or a graph.

For example, as shown below, the table of values for the function $f(x) = x^2$ and the graph for $f(x) = 7x$ could be compared to see which grows faster when x increases in size.

Input	Output
1	1
2	4
3	9
4	16

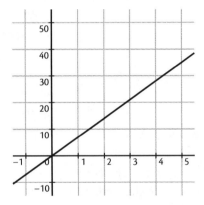

The table shows that $f(x) = x^2$ increases by larger and larger values as x increases, but the graph shows that $f(x) = 7x$ grows more consistently, always by 7 for an increase of 1 in x. Thus, it is clear that the first function grows more quickly as x gets larger.

Students should recognize the difference between growth that is long run versus short run. Mathematically, long-term growth is usually of more interest.

➤ *Qualitative features of functions.* Students might spend some time exploring non-linear functions such as $f(x) = 3x^2$ or $f(x) = 2x + x^2$ to see how the values of the dependent variable increase and decrease. They could notice, first of all, that the functions are not linear because their graphs are curved (not straight lines) and that their tables of values do not show constant increases. Students might also look for areas of increase and decrease.

For example, consider $f(x) = 2x + x^2$, which is graphed at the top of the next page:

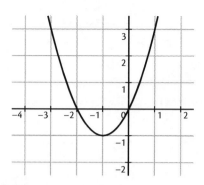

The function decreases as x increases until $x = -1$, and then it starts increasing. Students might analyze why this observation makes sense. When x is negative and far from 0, the x^2 term matters most, and it is positive. But for fractions near $x = 0$, the x^2 term is less than $2x$, and so the negative term matters most, explaining the y-values being negative. As x becomes positive, the function increases, because both x^2 and $2x$ increase, contributing to the increase in the dependent variable.

Good Questions to Ask

* Which of these do you think is a function? Why?

  * Triple a number and then subtract half of it.
  * Take a number away from 20.
  * Add three times a number to its square.
  * Take the square root of four times the number.

  [**Answer (example):** The first three are functions, since when you follow the rule with any number, you get a specific answer. The last one is not a function, since you could get more than one output for a single input. If, for example, the input were 9, the output could be either 6 or −6.]

* Choose a measurement formula and tell whether and why you do or do not think it implicitly describes a function. [**Answer (examples):**

  * The formula $A = \pi r^2$ is a function, since the input is the value of r and the output is the area of the circle. There is only one area for any circle. The inputs have to be positive numbers only, though, or there wouldn't really be a circle.
  * The formula $A = bh$ for the area of a parallelogram is a function if the input is a pair of numbers (b and h) and the output is the area. Both b and h have to be non-negative.]

* Describe a function in which many inputs lead to the same output. [**Answer (examples):**

  * The function could be the distance of a number from 0 on the number line. Any number except 0 and its opposite have the same output.

• The function could be the greatest integer less than the value of a number. So, if the input were any mixed number between 2 and 3, there would be the same output of 2.]

• Suppose the input were an area measure and the output were a shape. Could that be a function? [**Answer:** No, because there are always a whole lot of shapes with any particular area. There would even be a whole lot of rectangles with the same area if you made the length smaller when you made the width greater.]

• Describe each function below using a different representation (verbal, table of values, graph, or symbolic). Tell what each representation makes easier to see about the function.

  • $f(x) = 10 - x$
  • Triple a number, subtract 10, and then double the result
  • A function whose graph looks like this one:

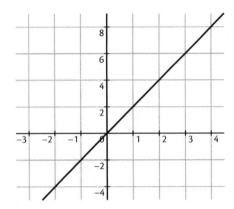

• A function that is described by this table of values:

Input	Output
1	−3
2	0
3	3
4	6

[**Answer (examples):**

• Another way to show $10 - x$ is to say "take a number away from 10." Both ways make it really easy to see that if x is a small number, the output is close to 10. I think the first way makes it easier to see that it's not the same as $x - 10$ since I could just do the algebra.

• Another way to write "triple a number, subtract 10, and then double the result" is $f(x) = 2(3x - 10)$. I think the first way makes it easier for me to get the output since I just follow the rules in order. For the other way, I need to know the rules for the order of math operations. But the second way makes it easier to see that the graph is going to be a line.

♦ Another way to describe the function shown in the graph is to make a table of values using ordered pairs taken from the graph. I think the table of values makes it easy to see that the value of the output increases by 2 when the value of the input increases by 1. But the graph makes it easy to see that the function is actually a line.

♦ Another way to express the table of values is by using the rule $f(x) = 3x - 6$, and I think the rule is better for figuring out what happens when x is not a whole number. But I think the table makes it easy to see that the value of the output increases by 3 when the value of the input increases by 1.]

• Describe a function that grows faster than $f(x) = 5x$. [**Answer (examples):**

♦ I would pick $f(x) = 7x$, since it goes up by 7s when the original function goes up by 5s.

♦ I would pick $f(x) = 5x^2$, since when x gets larger, $5x^2$ becomes a lot larger than x.]

• How would using a table of values help you figure out how fast a function grows? [**Answer (example):** I would pick a consistent value for the increase of the inputs and then look at how the outputs increase for that consistent input value change.]

• How do you know that the function $f(x) = 4 - 3x - 2x^2$ increases when x increases sometimes, but not all the time. [**Answer (examples):**

♦ I graphed it and that's what I saw.

♦ When $x = -10$, $f(x) = -166$, but when $x = 0$, $f(x) = 4$, which is an increase. But when $x = 10$, $f(x) = -226$, which is a decrease from the result when $x = 0$.

♦ When x is negative and far from 0, the output will be a large negative number. When $x = 0$, the output is 4. But when x is positive and far from 0, the output will be a large negative number. So that is an increase and then a decrease in the output as the input increases.]

Linear Functions

Functions	CCSSM 8.F

Use functions to model relationships between quantities.

4. Construct a function to model a linear relationship between two quantities. Determine the rate of change and initial value of the function from a description of a relationship or from two (x, y) values, including reading these from a table or from a graph. Interpret the rate of change and initial value of a linear function in terms of the situation it models, and in terms of its graph or a table of values.

5. Describe qualitatively the functional relationship between two quantities by analyzing a graph (e.g., where the function is increasing or decreasing, linear or nonlinear). Sketch a graph that exhibits the qualitative features of a function that has been described verbally.

IMPORTANT UNDERLYING IDEAS

> *Using linear functions to describe relationships.* The ideas in the section on Equations of Lines (pages 113–121) describing proportional relationships, slope, and so forth can all be reframed using the language of functions. For example, the relationship $y = 60x$, which relates the number of minutes (y) to the number of hours (x), can be reframed as a function $f(x) = 60x$. The input is the number of hours and the output is the number of minutes. The unit rate, which is the slope of the line, appears as the coefficient of x in the function, just as it would in the equation of the line. The relationship $y = 100 + 10x$, which might describe the cost (y) of a gym membership that has an initial fee of $100 and a monthly charge of $10, could be described by the function $f(x) = 100 + 10x$, where x is the number of months of membership.

If students construct tables of values to describe linear functions, they will notice that there is a constant increase in the values for one variable if there is a constant increase for the other. Some students tend to choose values of the independent variable randomly when they construct a table of values and might never notice the consistency in the increase of the dependent variable. A consistent increase of, for example, 1 can be applied to the independent variable, producing a progression such as $x = 1$, then 2, then 3, then 4, . . . , but an increase of any size, applied consistently, could be informative. For example, the increase could be a constant 2 or even a constant $\frac{1}{2}$ or $-\frac{1}{2}$.

Students should have opportunities to work with tables of values in which the values of the independent variable do not increase in a constant way, for example, a table for the function $f(x) = 3x$. In a case such as this, students will see how it becomes harder to recognize what is going on.

x	f(x)
0	0
1	3
6	18
10	30

Students should associate the constant increase in the dependent variable of a linear function when the independent variable increases by 1 with the unit rate describing the relationship being graphed. They should also note that sometimes the values of the dependent variable are multiples of the corresponding values of the independent variable, but they should be aware that sometimes an initial constant value is added to that multiple of the independent variable.

For example, the function below, which describes the number of legs possessed by a given number of healthy dogs, is one in which not only is the increase in the dependent variable constant but also, because the variables are proportional, the value of the dependent variable is the product of that increase and the corresponding value of the independent variable. In this case, the number of legs is a multiple of 4.

Dogs	Legs
1	4
2	8
3	12
4	16

But in some situations, the dependent variable is not a simple multiple of the independent variable. For example, the table below shows the relationship between how much a person has in the bank after so many weeks and the number of weeks if the person started with $48 and put in $5 a week.

Weeks	Amount in bank
0	48
1	53
2	58
3	63
4	68
5	73

There is a constant increase of 5 in the amount in the bank, but the amount values are not the products of 5 and the number of weeks or multiples of 5.

However, if one more column were added to the table, the student could see that if what is called the "initial value," 48 (the value when *weeks* = 0), is subtracted from the value of the dependent variable, the new column looks much like the legs column in the dogs/legs table. In effect, the weeks column and the newly added column form a multiplication table, as shown below.

Weeks	Amount in bank	Amount in bank less 48
0	48	0
1	53	5
2	58	10
3	63	15
4	68	20
5	73	25

It becomes clear that the function describing the amount after x weeks is $f(x) = 5x + 48$.

Since the unit rate (or rate of increase in the dependent variable for an increase of 1 in the independent variable) applies anywhere in a table of values, it is important that students realize that they can subtract any two values of the dependent variable and divide the result by the difference between the corresponding independent variables to determine that unit rate. For example, students can see that the unit increase is

$$\frac{53 - 48}{1 - 0} = \frac{5}{1} = 5.$$

But using the third and fourth rows, students get the same value, that is,

$$\frac{63 - 58}{3 - 2} = \frac{5}{1} = 5.$$

Even when using non-adjacent rows, such as the second and the sixth rows, the same value is achieved, that is,

$$\frac{73 - 53}{5 - 1} = \frac{20}{4} = \frac{5}{1} = 5.$$

This is because the increase of 4 in the independent variable matches a 4×5 increase for the dependent variable; the unit rate is still 5.

Students could plot the points appearing in a table of values such as this one to see that the process of determining the rate is the same in both formats. On the graph, dividing the rise of the line (the increase or decrease in the value of the dependent variable) by the run (the increase or decrease in the value of the independent variable), to get the slope of the line, is the same as subtracting the y values on two rows in the table (which correspond to the y-coordinates of two points on the line) and dividing them by the difference between the x values on those two rows in the table (which correspond to the x-coordinates for the two points on the line).

> **Describing types of linear functions.** Students should explore different ways to define linear functions and how they interrelate.

According to one definition, a linear function is one whose graph is a line. This requirement could be the starting point from which students discover that the equation of the line always takes the form $f(x) = ax + b$, that there is always an initial value equal to b (when $a = 0$), and that subsequent values always increase (or decrease) in a constant way by multiples of a.

Another definition states that a linear function is one whose equation is of the form $f(x) = ax + b$. Students would discover that the graphs of such equations are always lines, that there is always an initial value equal to b (when $a = 0$), and that subsequent values always increase (or decrease) in a constant way by multiples of a.

Or the definition could be that a function describes a relationship in which there is an initial value called "b" and that subsequent values increase (or decrease) in a constant way by multiples of a value called "a". Students learn that the graph of this relationship is a line and that the equation of the line is of the form $f(x) = ax + b$. So, if a table of values with $x = 1, 2, 3, 4, \ldots$ has corresponding values that grow by 3, then 8, then 12, etc., the graph cannot be a line.

To help students gain a thorough understanding of linear functions, each of these three approaches to definition should be considered.

When exploring these relationships, students should note that sometimes functions are increasing (eventually realizing that this occurs when a is positive), sometimes decreasing (eventually realizing that this occurs when a is negative), and sometimes increasing (or decreasing) more quickly or less quickly (depending on how great the absolute value of a is).

Students should recognize that if they are asked to create a linear function that increases quickly, something like $f(x) = 25x + 3$ makes sense, but if they want a linear function that decreases slowly, something like $f(x) = -0.5x + 9$ makes sense.

Students should explore the fact that the value of the b tells them what is called the "y-intercept," which is the initial value in the relationship because that is the value when there is a 0 value (therefore, initial) for the independent variable. As part of this exploration, they might be asked to consider what the equation of a line might be if it has a negative initial value (realizing that it might be, for example, $f(x) = 4x - 8$) or if it has a large positive initial value (realizing that it might be, for example, $f(x) = 2x + 30$).

The teacher could also initiate a discussion about why a linear function that is defined for all real number inputs always goes through either two or three quadrants of the coordinate plane and never one or four. Students could observe that the line cannot go through only one quadrant because the inputs are all real numbers, so the line has to extend infinitely to the right and left (or up and down). They should also realize that it cannot go through all four quadrants since that would require both an increase somewhere and a decrease somewhere, and linear functions either constantly increase or constantly decrease.

Good Questions to Ask

* What makes a function linear? Why? [**Answer (examples):** That when you graph it, you get a line, since "line" is part of the word "linear." **OR** That when you increase the input by 1, the output always increases by a constant amount.]
* The unit rate in a proportional relationship is 25. What might the relationship be? What would the table of values, graph, and equation look like? [**Answer (example):**
  * It could be how many cents different numbers of quarters are worth. The equation of the relationship would be $f(x) = 25x$. In the table of values, the outputs would look like a table of multiplication by 25. The graph would be a really steep line through the origin.
  * It could be a relationship with the equation $f(x) = 200 + 25x$, which would tell how much money is in a bank account that started with $200 and then had $25 added every week for x weeks. In the table of values, the amount would increase by 25 every time x increases by 1, but when $x = 0$, the amount would be 200. The graph would be a line that has an intercept of (0,200) and is really steep.]
* If a linear function increases slowly, what do you notice about its equation? What if it decreases quickly? [**Answer (example):** If the function increases slowly, the coefficient of x would be pretty small and it would be positive. If it decreases quickly, the coefficient of x would be a negative number really far from 0.]
* Another linear function, graphed on the same coordinate grid as $f(x) = 3x - 8$, is much steeper than $f(x) = 3x - 8$ and does not go through all the same quadrants. What might the function be? How do you know? [**Answer (example):** $f(x) = -20x + 8$. I know my function goes through Quadrant II, for example, when $x = -10$. But $f(x) = 3x - 8$ never goes into Quadrant II since, if x is negative, $f(x)$ is too, so the points are in Quadrant III, not II.]

* Which of these statements do you think is true and why?
    * A linear function with a negative slope has to go through Quadrants I, II, and IV.
    * A linear function with a negative slope might go through Quadrants I, II, and IV.

    [**Answer (example):** I know the first statement is false since $f(x) = -x$ goes through Quadrants I and III only. I know the second statement is true since $f(x) = -20x + 10$ goes through Quadrant II when $x = -2$, through Quadrant I when $x = \frac{1}{4}$, and through Quadrant IV when $x = 10$.]

* What does the initial value of a linear function represent? [**Answer (examples):** It tells what the value of the function is when the input is 0. **OR** It is the value of b when $f(x) = mx + b$. **OR** It is the y-intercept when you graph the function.]

Pythagorean Theorem

Geometry	CCSSM 8.G

Understand and apply the Pythagorean Theorem.	

7. Apply the Pythagorean Theorem to determine unknown side lengths in right triangles in real-world and mathematical problems in two and three dimensions.
8. Apply the Pythagorean Theorem to find the distance between two points in a coordinate system.

IMPORTANT UNDERLYING IDEAS

➤ **Thinking of the Pythagorean Theorem algebraically.** The Pythagorean Theorem has geometric, numeric, and algebraic aspects. The geometric aspect has to do with the areas of squares that are built on the sides of a right triangle. The numeric aspect has to do with calculating two sides when the third is known. But the algebraic aspect involves thinking of the theorem as generalized arithmetic and a tool, when algebraic techniques are applied, to determine a missing side length.

For example, knowing that the hypotenuse of a right triangle is 20" and one side is 10" allows a student to solve the equation $10^2 + s^2 = 20^2$ to determine the missing side length.

As well, the Pythagorean Theorem can be applied in a number of other algebraic situations. At the 8th-grade level, it can be used to determine the distance between two points on a coordinate grid. Knowing the difference between the x-coordinates and the difference between the y-coordinates provides the lengths of two sides of a right triangle; the piece of line whose distance is required is the hypotenuse.

For example, the distance between (1,5) and (3,11) on the line $y = 3x + 2$ is determined in this way:

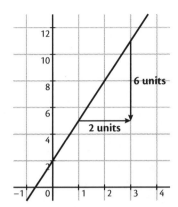

The hypotenuse length is $\sqrt{2^2 + 6^2} = 2\sqrt{10}$. Students should notice that the vertical distance is 3 times the horizontal distance because the slope of the line is 3.

Later, students can use the Pythagorean Theorem to represent equations of the form $x^2 + y^2 = 100$. At this level, as will be discussed below, students can use the Pythagorean Theorem to solve equations related to various measurement situations.

Good Questions to Ask

• What equations could you write to describe each situation? What would a solution be? If there is more than one possibility, write several equations and solve them.

  ◆ Two side lengths of a right triangle are 10" and 12". What could the length of the third side be?
  ◆ One side of a right triangle is half the length of another side, and the hypotenuse is 10". What could the lengths of the three sides be?

  [*Answer (examples)*:

  ◆ For the first situation, if the unknown side is the hypotenuse, $10^2 + 12^2 = h^2$, and the solution is $\sqrt{244}$. **OR** If the unknown side is one of the legs, $10^2 + s^2 = 12^2$, and the solution is $\sqrt{44}$.
  ◆ For the second situation, if one leg is double the other, $s^2 + (2s)^2 = 10^2$, so the lengths would be $2\sqrt{5}$, $4\sqrt{5}$, and 10. **OR** If the hypotenuse is double one of the legs, that leg would be 5 and the other leg would be $5\sqrt{3}$.]

• Choose the equation of a line. Then choose two points on the line in two different quadrants. Tell how far apart they are along that line. Explain all your thinking. [*Answer (example)*: $y = 4x - 8$ is my line. Two points are (−1,−12) and (4,8). The distance between them is $\sqrt{5^2 + 20^2}$, which is $5\sqrt{17}$. I used the Pythagorean

Theorem. Side lengths of the triangle I looked at were 5 and 20, and I figured out the length of the hypotenuse to get the distance between my two points.]

* Use the Pythagorean Theorem to describe two points that are 5 units apart on each line below:

$$y = 3x - 4$$
$$2y = 5x + 11$$

[**Answer (examples):**

* For $y = 3x - 4$, I know that the difference in y values is triple the distance in x values, so the equation to solve is $s^2 + (3s)^2 = 25$. That means $10s^2 = 25$, or $s^2 = 2.5$, which gives $s = 1.58$, so any two x values 1.58 apart would work. I used $(0,-4)$ and $(1.58,0.74)$.
* For $2y = 5x + 11$, the slope is 5/2, so the difference in y values is 2.5 times the difference in x values. The equation to solve is $s^2 + (2.5s)^2 = 25$. That means $7.25s^2 = 25$, or $s^2 = 3.45$, which gives $s = 1.86$, so any two x values 1.86 apart would work. I used $(0,5.5)$ and $(1.86,10.15)$.]

Measurement Problems

Geometry	CCSSM 8.G
Solve real-world and mathematical problems involving volume of cylinders, cones, and spheres.	

9. Know the formulas for the volumes of cones, cylinders, and spheres and use them to solve real-world mathematical problems.

IMPORTANT UNDERLYING IDEAS

> **Formulas for volumes of cones, cylinders, and spheres.** Measurement formulas are equations that relate different variables. For example, the formula $V = \pi r^2 h$ is an equation that is true for the values of V, r, and h for any particular cylinder. If two of the values are known, the equation can be used to determine the third. For example, if the volume of a cylinder is 106.3 cubic inches and the radius is 2 inches, then the height must be $\frac{106.3}{4\pi}$ inches.

At this level, the formulas that might be considered include

$$V_{cone} = \frac{1}{3}\pi r^2 h$$
$$V_{cylinder} = \pi r^2 h$$
$$V_{sphere} = \frac{4}{3}\pi r^3$$

Using measurement formulas is a very useful way to practice algebraic skills. It helps students not only to calculate measurements but also to see how variables are related in realistic situations.

Good Questions to Ask

* Ask students for an equation to model this measurement problem: The radius of a sphere was doubled. What happened to the volume? [*Answer (example):* The volume of the small sphere is $V = \frac{4}{3}\pi r^3$. The volume of the big sphere is

$$V = \frac{4}{3}\pi(2r)^3$$
$$= \frac{32}{3}\pi r^3$$
$$= 8(\frac{4}{3}\pi r^3).$$

So the volume of the small sphere was multiplied by 8.]

* Ask students for an equation to model this measurement problem: The radius of a cone increased by 10" and the height did not change. What happened to the volume? [*Answer (example):* The volume of the original cone is $V = \frac{1}{3}\pi r^2 h$. That means the volume of the new cone is

$$\frac{1}{3}\pi(r + 10)^2 h = \frac{1}{3}\pi(r^2 + 20r + 100)h$$
$$= \frac{1}{3}\pi r^2 h + \frac{20}{3}\pi rh + \frac{100}{3}\pi h$$
$$= \text{old volume} + \frac{20}{3}\pi rh + \frac{100}{3}\pi h$$
$$= \text{old volume} + \frac{20}{3}\pi h(r + 5).$$

So the increase in volume was $\frac{20}{3}\pi h(r + 5)$. The amount of increase depends on both the original radius and the original height.]

* Ask students to create a measurement problem involving the volume of a cylinder. Then ask them to create and solve an equation that would model the problem. [*Answer (example):* A can had a volume of 100 cm³. What might the radius and height have been? Since the volume of a cylinder is $V = \pi r^2 h$, one possible solution is $r = 10$ cm and $h = \frac{1}{\pi}$.]

Linear Trends

Statistics and Probability	CCSSM 8.SP
Investigate patterns of association in bivariate data.	

2. Know that straight lines are widely used to model relationships between two quantitative variables. For scatter plots that suggest a linear association, informally fit a straight line, and informally assess the model fit by judging the closeness of the data points to the line.

3. Use the equation of a linear model to solve problems in the context of bivariate measurement data, interpreting the slope and intercept. For example, in a linear model for a biology experiment, interpret a slope of 1.5 cm/hr as meaning that an additional hour of sunlight each day is associated with an additional 1.5 cm in mature plant height.

IMPORTANT UNDERLYING IDEAS

> ➤ *Lines of best fit.* Sometimes students gather data to attempt to derive a relation-ship between two variables. If, when those data are plotted, the relationship looks "almost" linear, the student might construct a line of best fit that would allow them to predict the value of one of the variables in terms of the other for unknown val-ues of the variables.

For example, imagine that a student gathered data about heights of high school boys and their fathers.

Boy height (in inches)	Dad height (in inches)
64	67
67	74
59	65
63	71
70	74
58	65
65	71

When graphed, a line can be used to "estimate" the points, as shown on the next page.

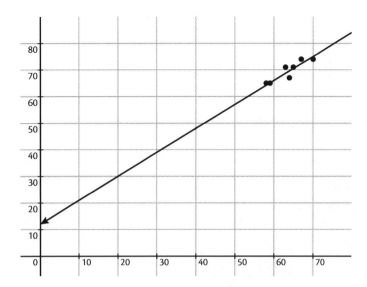

Looking at the graph, it appears to have a slope of about 0.9 and an intercept of about 12. Students can draw a line, using a ruler, that seems to fit the points best. That line is usually above some points and below others; it is certainly not below all of them or above all of them. Ideally, the line is close to many points.

In this case, the line drawn might have the equation $y = 0.9x + 12$. Using that relationship, one can predict the height of the father of a boy who is any height. For example, one might predict the height of the father of a boy who is 68" tall to be about 73" tall. This equation is just an estimate. There is a procedure for getting the best estimate called "linear regression" and a procedure for determining how good that fit is, but these procedures are not examined yet at the 8th-grade level.

Since the slope of the line is about 0.9, that suggests that if a boy is 1" taller than another, the taller boy's father is about 0.9" taller than the shorter boy's father.

It is important that students understand that the point of creating a line of best fit is primarily for predicting unknown values but also for understanding more deeply how the variables are related (e.g., really understanding how a certain increase in the independent variable affects the increase in the dependent variable). Students should realize that the equation for the line of best fit may or may not yield the values that actually appear in the original table.

Good Questions to Ask

• The table below shows how quickly a runner can cover certain distances. Describe the equations for two reasonable lines of best fit for the data. What would the time likely be for 225 m? What does the slope of the line represent?

Distance (m)	50	100	150	200	250
Time (s)	6.3	12.7	19.1	25.6	32.1

[*Answer (example):* $y = 0.13x - 0.2$ **OR** $y = 0.126x + 0.2$. The likely time for 225 m in the first case would be about 29.1 s. The slope tells how much farther the runner gets in 1 second.]

• Why might it be hard to find a good line of fit for these data?

X	5	15	25	35	45
Y	1,000	800	225	2,000	10

[*Answer (example):* Because the points don't really seem to lie on a line. Sometimes the values go up a lot and sometimes less; sometimes they go up and sometimes they go down.]

• Create a set of data for which $y = -2x + 9$ might be a reasonable line of best fit. [*Answer (example):* A table of values for some possible data is shown below.]

x	0	5	10	15	20
y	8	−4	−10	−22	−30

Summary

By the end of Grade 8, students should use algebraic generalizations to work with powers. They should deeply understand the concept of a function, and, in particular, of linear functions. They should have a sense of what the slope and intercept of a line tell us and which situations are described by linear relationships. They can connect equations of a line with associated tables of values and graphs. They can also describe situations requiring the simultaneous solution of two linear equations in two unknowns. They can solve linear equations by using a variety of techniques and use equations to solve measurement problems.

CONCLUSION

MANY TEACHERS were simply never taught many of the strategies to which they could expose their students to most effectively help those students develop a better grasp of algebraic concepts. I hope this resource provides some of that valuable mathematical background for the classroom teacher working with instruction in algebra.

The Good Questions provided in each section are only samples of what could be asked. What is important about the particular types of questions presented here is that many of them foster higher-level thinking and evoke the mathematical practice standards that are critical in today's math classroom. The more teachers can get students to not just arrive at solutions, but to really think about mathematical ideas, the better off the students will be. The sample questions provided in this resource almost all require students to *think* about the math, not just do it.

BIBLIOGRAPHY

Arcavi, A. (1994). Symbol sense: Informal sense-making in formal mathematics. *For the Learning of Mathematics, 14*(3), 24–35.

Asquith, P., Stephens, A. C., Knuth, E. J., & Alibali, M. W. (2007). Middle school mathematics teachers' knowledge of students' understanding of core algebraic concepts: Equal sign and variable. *Mathematical Thinking and Learning, 9*(3), 249–272.

Booth, L. R. (1988). Children's difficulties in beginning algebra. In A. F. Coxford & A. P. Shulte (Eds.), *The idea of algebra, K–12* (pp. 20–32). Reston, VA: National Council of Teachers of Mathematics.

Cai, J., & Knuth, E. J. (2005). Introduction: The development of students' algebraic thinking in earlier grades from curricular, instructional and learning perspectives. *ZDM—The International Journal on Mathematics Education, 37*(1), 1–4.

Carpenter, T. P., Franke, M. L., & Levi, L. (2003). *Thinking mathematically: Integrating arithmetic and algebra in elementary school.* Portsmouth, NH: Heinemann.

Christou, K. P., Vosniadou, S., & Vamvakoussi, X. (2007). Students' interpretations of literal symbols in algebra. In S. Vosniadou, A. Baltas, & X. Vamvakoussi (Eds.), *Re-framing the conceptual change approach in learning and instruction* (pp. 285–299). Oxford, UK: Elsevier.

Dole, S. (2010). Making connections to the big ideas in mathematics: Promoting proportional reasoning. In C. Glascodine & K.-A. Hoad (Eds.), *Teaching mathematics? Make it count: What research tells us about effective teaching and learning of mathematics. ACER Research Conference 2010, Melbourne, Australia* (pp. 71–74). Camberwell, Australia: Australian Council for Educational Research. Available at research.acer.edu.au/cgi/viewcontent.cgi?article=1086&context=research_conference

Driscoll, M., & Moyer, J. (2001). Using students' work as a lens on algebraic thinking. *Mathematics Teaching for Middle School, 6*(5), 282–287.

Ellis, A. B. (2007). Connections between generalizing and justifying: Students' reasoning with linear relationships. *Journal for Research in Mathematics Education, 38*(3), 194–229.

Falle, J. (2007). Students' tendency to conjoin terms: An inhibition to their development of algebra. In J. Watson & K. Beswick (Eds.), *Mathematics: Essential research, essential practice. Proceedings of the 30th Annual Conference of the Mathematics Education Research Group of Australasia: Vol. 1* (pp. 285–294). Adelaide, Australia: MERGA.

Greenes, C. E., & Rubenstein, R. (Eds.). (2008). *Algebra and algebraic thinking in school mathematics.* Reston, VA: National Council of Teachers of Mathematics.

Hallagan, J. E. (2006). The case of Bruce: A teacher's model of her students' algebraic thinking about equivalent expressions. *Mathematics Education Research Journal, 18*(1), 103–123.

Humberstone, J., & Reeve, R. A. (2008). Profiles of algebraic competence. *Learning and Instruction, 18*, 254–367.

Jacobs, V. R., Franke, M. L., Carpenter, T. P., Levi, L., & Battey, D. (2007). Professional development focused on children's algebraic reasoning in elementary school. *Journal for Research in Mathematics Education, 38*(3), 258–288.

Johanning, D. I. (2004). Supporting the development of algebraic thinking in middle school: A closer look at students' informal strategies. *Journal of Mathematical Behavior, 23,* 371–388.

Kaput, J. J. (1995). A research base supporting long term algebra reform? In D. T. Owens, M. K. Reed, & G. M. Millsaps (Eds.), *Proceedings of the 17th annual meeting of the PME-NA: Vol. 1* (pp. 71–94). Columbus, OH: ERIC Clearinghouse for Science, Mathematics and Environmental Education.

Kaput, J. J. (1998). Teaching and learning a new algebra with understanding. Available at www.educ.fc.ul.pt/docentes/jponte/da/da-textos/kaput_99algund.pdf

Kieran, C. (1992). The learning and teaching of school algebra. In D. Grouws (Ed.), *Handbook of research on mathematics teaching and learning* (pp. 390–419). New York, NY: Macmillan.

Kieran, C. (1996). The changing face of school algebra. In C. Alcina, J. M. Alvares, B. Hodgson, C. Laborde, & A. Pérez (Eds.), *Proceedings of the Eighth International Congress on Mathematics Education: Selected Lectures* (pp. 271–290). Seville, Spain: S.A.E.M. Thales.

Kieran, C. (2004). Algebraic thinking in the early grades. *The Mathematics Educator, 8*(1), 139–151.

Knuth, E. J., Stephens, A. C., McNeil, N. M., & Alibali, M. W. (2006). Does understanding the equal sign matter? Evidence from solving equations. *Journal for Research in Mathematics Education, 37,* 297–312.

Linchevski, L., & Livneh, D. (1999). Structure sense: The relationship between algebraic and numerical contexts. *Educational Studies in Mathematics, 40,* 173–196.

MacGregor, M., & Stacey, K. (1993). Cognitive models underlying students' formulation of simple linear equations. *Journal for Research in Mathematics Education, 24*(3), 217–232.

Mason, J. (2005). *Developing thinking in algebra.* Thousand Oaks, CA: SAGE Publications.

National Council of Teachers of Mathematics. (2000). *Principles and standards for school mathematics.* Reston, VA: Author.

National Mathematics Advisory Panel. (2008). *Foundations for success: The final report of the National Mathematics Advisory Panel.* Washington, DC: U.S. Department of Education.

National Research Council. (2001). *Adding it up: Helping children learn mathematics.* Washington, DC: National Academies Press.

Norton, S., & Irvin, J. (2007). A concrete approach to teaching symbolic algebra. In J. Watson & K. Beswick (Eds.), *Mathematics: Essential research, essential practice. Proceedings of the 30th annual conference of the Mathematics Education Research Group of Australasia, Vol. 2* (pp. 551–560). Adelaide, Australia: MERGA.

Usiskin, Z. (1988). Conceptions of school algebra and uses of variables. In A. F. Coxford & A. P. Shulte (Eds.), *The ideas of algebra, K–12* (pp. 8–19). Reston, VA: National Council of Teachers of Mathematics.

Usiskin, Z. (1995). Why is algebra important? *American Educator, 19*(1), 30–37.

INDEX

INDEX OF SUBJECTS AND CITED AUTHORS

INDEX OF COMMON CORE STANDARDS IN MATHEMATICS

ABOUT THE AUTHOR

MARIAN SMALL is the former Dean of Education at the University of New Brunswick. She speaks regularly about differentiating instruction and asking better questions in K–12 mathematics.

She has been an author on many mathematics text series at both the elementary and the secondary levels. She has served on the author team for the National Council of Teachers of Mathematics (NCTM) Navigation series (pre-K–2), as the NCTM representative on the Mathcounts question writing committee for middle school mathematics competitions throughout the United States, and as a member of the editorial panel for the NCTM 2011 yearbook on motivation and disposition.

Dr. Small is probably best known for her books *Good Questions: Great Ways to Differentiate Mathematics Instruction* and *More Good Questions: Great Ways to Differentiate Secondary Mathematics Instruction* (with Amy Lin). *Eyes on Math: A Visual Approach to Teaching Math Concepts* was published in 2013, as was *Uncomplicating Fractions to Meet Common Core Standards in Math, K–7.* She is also author of the first and second editions of a text for university preservice teachers and practicing teachers, *Making Math Meaningful to Canadian Students: K–8*, as well as the professional resources *Big Ideas from Dr. Small: Grades 4–8; Big Ideas from Dr. Small: Grades K–3;* and *Leaps and Bounds toward Math Understanding: Grades 3–4, Grades 5–6,* and *Grades 7–8*, all published by Nelson Education Ltd.

She led the research resulting in the creation of maps describing student mathematical development in each of the five NCTM mathematical strands for the K–8 levels and has created the associated professional development program, PRIME.